AF439159

WRITE IT OFF!

AN AUTHOR'S GUIDE TO

BOOKKEEPING AND TAXES

CHRISTY NICHOLAS, CPA

GREEN DRAGON PUBLISHING

TABLE OF CONTENTS

Introduction

You've poured your soul into your writing. Now, let's make sure you keep as much of your hard-earned income as possible.

Whether you're a seasoned author with a library full of bestsellers or a novice with one manuscript and a dream, this book is your friendly companion in the world of financial jargon, bookkeeping chaos, and tax tangles.

If you can handle a plot twist, you can handle your finances with a bit of flair. Before diving into the wonderful world of bookkeeping and taxes for authors, let's get the caveats and provisos out of the way:

•   While this guide is here to entertain and inform, it's not official financial advice.

•   We're targeting writers based in the United States, but many of the bookkeeping tips and tricks can be useful to authors in other countries.

- Please remember that tax laws are as fickle as a soap opera plot twist. They can change at any moment.

- While this guide aims to help you navigate the financial seas, always check for the latest updates or consult a real-life tax professional if you're about to sign on the dotted line.

Throughout the chapters, you'll find exercises to help turn theory into practice. So, grab your pen, your favorite coffee, and let's turn these tax trials into plot twists you can master.

Chapter One

Setting the Scene

What's Your Story?

Welcome to the wonderful world of words, where every author dreams of crafting bestsellers and sipping coffee in quaint cafés while writing the next great novel.

Before you get too cozy with your quill (or keyboard), there's a plot twist to untangle. *Taxes and bookkeeping:* words to strike fear in the heart of most creative types. This is the unglamorous but absolutely essential side of being a self-published author.

You might be wondering, "Why on earth should I care about taxes? I'm an author, not an accountant!" But like it or not, every sale comes with financial responsibilities. It's not all about conjuring up captivating characters or crafting cliffhangers. It's also about keeping the taxman happy and making sure you're not missing out on the deductions you deserve.

I'm here to help you navigate the financial labyrinth so you can keep writing without fearing the dreaded Infernal Revenue Service lurking in the shadows.

Tax Tales: Navigating Obligations for Authors

You've just published your first book. The sales are rolling in, fans are showering you with praise, and everything seems perfect. Then, tax season arrives, and suddenly, you're staring at a mountain of paperwork with terms like "Schedule C," "1099," and "deductions" that might as well be in an ancient, forgotten language.

You're not alone. Many authors are blindsided by the complexities of taxes and bookkeeping, especially when they realize they're not just hobbyists but bona fide small business owners.

So, why can't we just pretend taxes don't exist? As much as we'd all love to ignore tax obligations like an unsolicited sequel to a bad movie, they're crucial for a few reasons.

First, failing to file or pay taxes can lead to hefty fines and penalties. That's not the kind of drama you want in your life.

Second, proper tax management can actually save you money. By understanding which expenses you can deduct and how to structure your business, you can keep more of your hard-earned royalties.

And third, having a proper understanding of the requirements and terminology can really help tone down the anxiety about taxes and bookkeeping. With a few tools and a bit of study, you can wrestle this feral monster into a manageable pet.

The Importance of Tax Management: Avoiding the Plot Twist You Don't Want

Imagine taxes as the villain in your story. They're not inherently evil, but they sure can be a nuisance if you're not prepared. And sometimes, there's even a redemption arc, and the villain turns into a reluctant ally.

Taxes may be the villain, but with the right preparation, you can write the ending.

Proper tax management is your secret weapon, your plot armor if you will. It helps you anticipate challenges, avoid costly mistakes, and navigate the intricate maze of rules and regulations. Think of it as world-building for your financial life. Every decision you make adds a layer to your story, setting the stage for success or potential pitfalls.

I'm not here to turn you into a tax wizard overnight, nor will I drown you in accounting jargon. I'm here to demystify taxes and bookkeeping so you can focus on your craft while confidently managing your finances.

I'll walk you through the essentials, from choosing the right business structure to understanding your income streams and mastering the art of deductions. Plus, I'll throw in some real-world examples and workbook exercises because, let's face it, taxes are way easier to learn if you can get your feet wet. Or hands. Whatever.

Whether you're a seasoned author with multiple titles under your belt or a newbie navigating your first book launch, this journey into the financial side of writing will equip you with the knowledge and tools to manage your money like a pro. You might even find yourself enjoying it. Let's dive in and turn those tax nightmares into a story with a happy ending.

Chapter Two

The Plot Thickens: Choosing Your Business Structure

As an author, you're already familiar with creating worlds, building characters, and weaving intricate plots. But there's one story element you might not have considered yet: your business structure. While it may seem like a trivial detail, this choice can have a significant impact on how you manage your income, expenses, and, yes, taxes. Grab your metaphorical quill and let's delve into the world of business structures, where risk and reward are the main characters.

Risk and Rewards: The Liability Chronicles

Every great story has its risks, and choosing your business structure is no different. Before you decide, consider how much risk you're willing to take on. Are you comfortable venturing into a world where your personal assets might be at stake, or would you prefer paying a bit more for extra protection?

Once you answer those questions, you're better positioned to make a decision. But don't let that be your only decision point, as you can also hedge your bets either way by purchasing strong business liability insurance.

Let's explore the different paths you can take.

A Solo Adventure: Sole Proprietorship

If you're the lone wolf type, the sole proprietorship might sound appealing. It's the simplest and most straightforward business structure, with no need for fancy paperwork or state filings. Just you, your pen (or keyboard), and your creative genius. However, this simplicity comes with a big catch called unlimited liability.

In a sole proprietorship, your business isn't a separate entity from you, meaning you're personally responsible for any debts or lawsuits. That could include claims on your home, car, or prized Tolkien first editions. Why would they sue an author? They may think you libeled them in a biopic. They may have relied on your advice in a tax guide. Or they may have tripped over a stack of books you had next to your table at an author signing. Whatever the reason, in this litigation-happy society we live in, it's something to keep in mind.

The upside to a sole proprietorship? There's no need for separate tax returns for the business. Everything flows through your personal tax return on a Schedule C. This simplicity extends to startup costs and annual maintenance, which can be practically none.

The downside? When you shuffle off this mortal coil, so does your business. The sole proprietorship is inextricably tied to your lifespan, so if your dream is for your publishing company to live on without you, choose another format.

Corporate Climax: Corporation

For those willing to pay a bit more for peace of mind, a Corporation offers the allure of limited liability. This means that the Corporation is a separate legal entity from you, and your personal assets are protected if things go awry. It's like having a magical barrier that shields your home and personal wealth from the perils of business lawsuits.

However, setting up a Corporation involves more than just waving a magic wand. There are setup fees, annual maintenance fees, and additional paperwork, such as filing a separate tax form (1120 or 1120S). The corporate tax rate can also be higher than personal tax rates, depending on the profits and the specific corporate structure chosen.

There are two main types of Corporations, each with very different structures: C Corporation and S Corporation.

C Corporation: Think big—Microsoft, Disney, IBM. A C Corporation pays taxes on profits, and then shareholders also pay taxes on dividends. This 'double taxation' can mean a higher tax burden.

S Corporation: A more modest option, perfect for small businesses. The S actually stands for 'Small.' S Corps avoid the double taxation fate by passing income directly to shareholders, who report it on their personal tax returns. That means the Corporation itself pays no income taxes, and the owners pay taxes at their personal income tax rate. However, there are restrictions, like a cap on the number of shareholders (100 max).

LLC Quest: Limited Liability Company

The Limited Liability Company (LLC) is the hybrid creature of the business world. Offering the best of both worlds, an LLC provides the limited liability of a Corporation with the tax simplicity of a sole proprietorship or Partnership. You get to keep your personal assets safe from business debts and lawsuits while enjoying a more straightforward tax situation.

LLCs offer flexibility. They can be single-member (you, solo) or multi-member (you and your co-author, perhaps). You can also choose how you want to be taxed, either as a sole proprietorship, a Partnership, or a Corporation. However, the rules governing LLCs can vary significantly from state to state, so it's wise to consult a CPA (Certified Public Accountant) or business law attorney who knows the local laws before settling on this choice. You can also use a registered agent, depending on where the LLC is based.

Partnership Playbook

If you're venturing into the literary world with a trusted partner, be it a spouse, friend, or fellow writer, a **Partnership** might be the way to go. Partnerships can be as simple as a handshake or as formal as a written agreement. A word of caution here: **always** get your Partnership terms in writing. Nothing sours a creative collaboration faster than money disputes.

In a Partnership, income and expenses are reported on a Partnership return (Form 1065), and each partner receives a Schedule K-1 that details their share of the profits and losses. These figures then flow through to the partners' personal tax returns. Like S Corps, Partnerships are not taxed at the business level, but on the individual partner's personal tax return.

Picking the Best Path

For most authors, a sole proprietorship is the most straightforward and cost-effective choice, especially if the risk of lawsuits is low. However, if your business involves significant liability—say, you're selling physical products or offering services that carry more risk—an LLC or an S Corporation might offer the best balance of protection and simplicity.

No matter which you prefer, you should research rules specific to the state you incorporate in for requirements before making a final choice.

As we continue, we'll assume you're leaning toward the sole proprietorship path, but we'll provide insights and tips that apply across all structures.

Choosing the right business structure is like picking the right genre for your book. It sets the tone for everything that follows. So, choose wisely, and let's keep writing your financial success story.

Workbook Exercise: Which Structure is the Best for your Writing Business?

This exercise will help you determine the most suitable business structure for your writing business. Consider your specific needs, goals, and potential risks. Answer the following questions honestly and thoroughly, then review your responses to identify the best option.

Step 1: Assess Your Needs and Goals

What is the primary focus of your writing business?
☐ Publishing books
☐ Freelance writing
☐ Selling physical products (merchandise, prints, etc.)
☐ Offering services (editing, coaching, workshops)
☐ Other: ___________________________________

___

Do you have any partners or co-authors involved in your business?
☐ Yes
☐ No

How much personal liability are you comfortable with?
☐ Low risk tolerance (Prefer personal asset protection)
☐ Moderate risk tolerance
☐ High risk tolerance (Comfortable with personal liability)

How complex do you want your tax filings to be?

☐ Simple (Minimal paperwork and reporting)
☐ Moderate (Willing to handle some complexity)
☐ Complex (Comfortable with more detailed filings)

Do you plan to reinvest your profits into the business or distribute them to owners?
☐ Reinvest profits
☐ Distribute profits to owners

How important is it to have a formal structure and legal separation between you and your business?
☐ Very important (Need legal separation)
☐ Somewhat important (Flexible but prefer some separation)
☐ Not important (Comfortable with informal structure)

Step 2: Consider Potential Risks

Does your business involve physical products or in-person services that could lead to potential lawsuits?
☐ Yes
☐ No

Do you have significant personal assets you want to protect from business liabilities?
☐ Yes
☐ No

How likely are you to take on debt or seek outside investment for your business?
☐ Very likely
☐ Somewhat likely
☐ Not likely

Step 3: Analyze Your Answers

Based on your answers, consider the following general guidance:

Sole Proprietorship: Best for those with high risk tolerance, minimal assets to protect, and a desire for simple tax filings. Ideal for authors and freelancers with minimal exposure to liability.

Partnership: Suitable if you have a co-author or business partner and are comfortable sharing profits and decision-making. Be sure to establish a formal Partnership agreement.

Limited Liability Company (LLC): Provides personal liability protection and flexibility in tax treatment. A good choice if you want to protect personal assets and have a formal business structure.

Corporation (C Corp or S Corp): Ideal for businesses planning to reinvest profits, seek investment, or take on debt. Offers strong liability protection and can be tax-efficient under certain circumstances.

Step 4: Make Your Decision

Based on the guidance above and your answers, which business structure seems the best fit for your writing business?

My chosen business structure:

____

Step 5: Next Steps

Research: Look into the specifics of your chosen structure, including state requirements and tax implications.

Consult Professionals: Consider consulting a CPA or business law attorney to confirm your choice and assist with setup. Verify that the professional has experience with authors and/or small business and works with your style. You can ask other authors for recommendations, too. (see Resources and Tools for more information on this process).

Implement: With the help of your chosen professional (if needed), take the necessary steps to establish your business structure, including filing any required paperwork and setting up appropriate record-keeping systems. See the Small Business Administration website for a step-by-step instruction on this (see the Appendix for a link)

By completing this exercise, you've taken a significant step toward structuring your writing business for success. Remember, the right business structure can provide a solid foundation, helping you manage risks and achieve your financial goals.

Chapter Three

Loving Your Ledger

If you're reading this book, chances are that you aren't an accountant. And that's perfectly fine! That's what the professionals are for. But, if you have a basic understanding of accounting terms, you might not have to pay one for doing the basics.

Set Up Your Chart of Accounts

It's time to create your Chart of Accounts. This is your cast of characters, each representing different aspects of your financial story:

• Assets: These are the things you own, such as your laptop or those royalties piling up in your bank account.

• Liabilities: The bills and debts your business has to pay to someone else. In other words, things you owe.

• Equity: This is what's left for you after paying off your liabilities, the true value of the company at this point in time.

• Revenue: This is the money you earn from book sales, speaking gigs, or those surprise bestseller moments.

• Expenses: These are costs like editing, printing, and marketing that you have to spend to keep your business running.

Record Your Transactions

Every time money changes hands, it's a new chapter in your business's financial story. You'll need to record each in what's called a Journal Entry.

There are two sides to each Journal Entry, a debit side and a credit side. Think of your bank account. Deposits are often shown in one column, while checks are shown in a different column.

In accounting, each type of account listed above has a 'normal balance' of either the debit side (left) or the credit side (right). Assets and Expenses are on the left, while Liabilities and Income are on the right. Equity should be on the right if the company is worth more than it owes.

For example:

<u>Assets:</u>
Cash: $1,000

<u>Liabilities:</u>
Loan on Computer: $200

<u>Equity:</u> $800
Totals: $1,000 $1,000

See? Each side balances.

For example, if you splurge on a shiny new author website for $500, you increase (debit) your expense account and decrease (credit) your cash balance.

Journal Entries are written so it's easy to see them visually.

Debit: Expense $500
      Credit: Cash $500

Post to the General Ledger

After you've recorded your journal entries, it's time to post them to the General Ledger. Each account has its own section in the ledger, and every transaction gets posted here, building the full narrative of your business's financial journey.

Reconcile Your Accounts

Every good story needs consistency, and that's what reconciliation is all about. Here, you'll compare your ledger accounts to your bank statements to make sure everything matches up.

Regular reconciliations ensure that your finances stay cohesive and error-free. Most banks will not correct an error if it's more than 60 days old, and credit cards have time limitations on disputing charges, so it's important to reconcile monthly.

Financial Statements

Once all your transactions are posted for the month, it's time to prepare your Financial Statements. These summarize how your business has been performing.

• The Income Statement (or Profit & Loss Statement) shows how much revenue you've earned versus the expenses you've faced. Did you end up with a profit (a bestseller) or a loss (back to the drawing board)?

• The Balance Sheet is a snapshot of your financial position at a specific point in time, listing your assets, liabilities, and equity. It helps you see how much your company is worth.

• The Cash Flow Statement details how cash is moving through your business, ensuring you've got the funds to keep writing your next book.

Congratulations, you've just set up a General Ledger for your author business! With this structure in place, you'll have a clear and organized financial narrative, helping you navigate the twists and turns of running a successful writing career. Now, back to crafting your next literary masterpiece!

Chapter Four

Income Quest: Understanding Your Writing Revenue

Defining the Loot: What Counts as Income?

Ah, income, the sweet, sweet payoff for all those late nights spent staring at a blinking cursor. But before you dive into that pile of cash (or, more realistically, that modest deposit in your bank account), let's get clear on what actually counts as income in the world of taxes. Spoiler alert: it's not just about money rolling in from every direction.

In the everyday world, "income" is any cash inflow, be it a loan from the bank, a paycheck from your day job, a generous gift from Grandma, or the spoils from selling a painting you whipped up on a whim. But when we step into the magical realm of accounting, "income" takes on a more precise definition. For you, intrepid author, it's all about the revenue from your primary business operations.

Translation: the dough you make from selling books and related writerly activities.

Let's break it down.

Primary Loot: Your Main Gig

Your bread and butter, your main storyline, this is where most of your income will come from. For authors, this usually means the sales of your books, whether they're gripping novels, insightful nonfiction, or quirky short stories. And don't forget the multiple formats. Physical copies, eBooks, and audiobooks all count.

Advances vs. Royalties

Welcome to the classic publishing dichotomy: advances and royalties. Think of advances as a signing bonus. It's the publisher's way of saying, "We believe in you, here's some cash upfront." But remember, it's not free money. It's an advance on future royalties, so don't spend it all on a celebratory dinner just yet.

• **Advances**: These are upfront payments you receive when you sign a publishing contract. They're recorded as income when the book is sent to the publisher. If an advance is paid before the book is complete, it's considered "unearned income" and hangs out in the "liability" section of your accounting ledger. Basically, money you might have to pay back if the manuscript never materializes.

•   **Royalties**: These are the payments that roll in (hopefully) after your advance has been "earned out," if you get no advance, or if you're self-published. That means once your book sales cover the advance amount, you start seeing royalties from each sale. Depending on whether you're using cash basis or accrual basis accounting, you'll record these either when you receive them or when they're earned. Check out Chapter Five for more on this thrilling topic.

Commissioned Chronicles: Personalized Earnings

Think of commissioned work as writing with a prompt, except the prompt is coming from someone willing to pay you. This could be anything from ghostwriting a memoir to crafting a bespoke story for a corporate event. Unlike selling pre-existing works, these projects are tailor-made to the client's specifications.

Just remember, this income doesn't get recorded until you've delivered the final product and satisfied the client. Until then, any upfront payments are liabilities, money you might have to give back if things go south.

Consignment Chronicles: Storefront Stories

Consignment sales are like a plot twist in your income narrative. You place your books or related products in someone else's store, and you only get paid when they sell. For example, if you have a book in a local bookstore on consignment for $30 and the store keeps $10 as their fee, you would report the $20 you receive as income. This means you only declare the amount you actually receive, not the total sale price.

You also have the option of reporting it on a gross basis. For instance, you may report the $30 total income but then deduct a $10 consignment fee.

Either method is acceptable to the IRS (Internal Revenue Service) as long as you remain consistent.

Grants and Scholarships

Many non-profit organizations offer help to artists in the form of grants and scholarships. While personal grants and scholarships are usually not taxable, some business grants might be subject to tax. The grant documentation would specify. In the case of scholarships, funds in excess of those used for tuition, fees, etc. might be taxable.

Crowdfunding Conundrum

Crowdfunding is like launching a book with a hype train already attached. Platforms like Kickstarter and Patreon let your fans fund your projects, but those funds are still taxable income. Whether you're pre-selling your book or offering exclusive content, keep track of what each supporter receives. It's crucial for classifying and taxing that income correctly. And don't forget to match your funds received with your expenses. More on that cliffhanger in Chapter Five.

Selling Sidequests

Sometimes, your writing life literally comes with extra baggage. Whether it's selling off extra supplies you never made into bookmarks or that old desk you've written a million words on, this is incidental income. It's not your main gig, but it still counts.

If you're offloading big-ticket items like a computer or display equipment, these might be classified as "gains" instead of regular income.

Shipping Shenanigans

Got a bunch of physical books to ship out? If you're charging for shipping, that's income too. You'll report the shipping fees as income, and the cost of shipping as an expense. Usually, these cancel each other out, but be careful not to jack up those shipping fees too high. You don't want to be that author with sky-high shipping costs scaring away potential readers.

Grants and Prizes

If you should be so fortunate as to be awarded either a writing grant or a prize, this would count as regular income, as it's directly related to your main business, writing.

Conclusion

In the grand narrative of your author business, income is any money you earn from your writing-related activities. It's important to distinguish this from other cash inflows like gifts or loans, which aren't taxable income.

By correctly identifying and reporting your income, you ensure you're only paying what you owe to the tax man; no more, no less. And remember, when in doubt, consult a tax professional. After all, no one wants a surprise plot twist with the IRS.

Workbook Exercise and Excel Sheet: Identifying Your Income Streams

To help you categorize and track the various sources of income from your writing business, ensuring accurate record-keeping and understanding of your financial situation.

Instructions:

List Your Income Sources:
o Write down all the potential sources of income related to your writing business. Think about book sales, commissioned work, consignment sales, crowdfunding, incidental sales, and any other relevant income streams.

Categorize Your Income:
o For each source, categorize the income into one of the following:
» Sales of books and related products
» Commissioned work
» Consignment sales
» Crowdfunding
» Incidental income

» Shipping fees

Determine the Nature of Each Income:
• Identify whether the income is earned (received after fulfilling a service/product) or unearned (received in advance but not yet earned).

Estimate Monthly Income:
• Estimate the monthly income you expect to receive from each source. If applicable, break down the income further into regular payments (e.g., royalties) versus one-time payments (e.g., advances).

Record Your Actual Income:
• Use the provided Excel sheet template to input your actual income as you receive it. Include the date, source, category, amount received, and any notes (e.g., for advances, note if the book has been delivered or not).

Analyze Your Income:
• At the end of the month, review your income streams. Note any discrepancies between expected and actual income, and identify patterns or areas for growth.

Excel Sheet Suggestions:

Income Tracking Sheet:

- Columns: Date, Source of Income, Category, Amount Received, Notes. Create a =SUM(X:X) formula to make totals at the bottom of each column.
- Categories: Sales, Commissioned Work, Consignment Sales, Crowdfunding, Incidental Income, Shipping Fees. You may also want to create a =SUM(X:X) formula to make totals at end of each line.

Commissioned Work Tracker:

- Columns: Project Name, Client, Agreed Fee, Deposit Received, Completion Date, Final Payment, Notes
- Details: Track the progress of commissioned projects, noting when deposits are received and final payments are due,

Crowdfunding Tracker:

- Columns: Platform (Kickstarter, Patreon, etc.), Campaign Name, Start Date, End Date, Total Funds Raised, Backer Rewards Fulfilled, Notes
- Details: Keep track of campaigns, amounts raised, and ensure backer rewards are fulfilled on time.

Expense and Shipping Tracker:

- Columns: Date, Description, Expense Type, Amount, Shipping Income, Shipping Expense, Notes
- Details: Track business-related expenses, including shipping costs and income, to calculate net profit accurately.

Yearly Income Summary:
• Columns: Month, Sales Income, Commissioned Income, Consignment Income, Crowdfunding Income, Incidental Income, Shipping Income, Total Income
• Formulas: Summarize monthly income across all categories to get an annual overview. Use charts to visualize trends and seasonal fluctuations.

Chapter Five

Expense Expedition

Welcome, brave author, to the perilous path of expense deductions. Navigating what you can and can't deduct is like plotting a multi-book series. One misstep, and you could land in a plot hole. Let's solve this financial mystery together to ensure your expense journey is smooth.

In this chapter, I'll start with expenses, then delve into fixed assets, those items that last more than a year like computers and desks. Then, I'll talk about cash basis vs. accrual basis.

Navigating Deductions: What Can You Deduct?

"Can I deduct this on my taxes?" The answer, like many things in life, is "it depends." But fear not, I'm here to help you sift through the clutter and find those golden deductions that can save you some serious coin. Now, onto the list of things you can deduct as a business expense. Think of these as the supporting characters in the great drama of your author career.

Advertising: Getting the Word Out

Whether it's designing a snazzy book cover, running ads on social media, or printing business cards, advertising expenses are fully deductible. So, feel free to plaster your face on every corner of the internet, and then deduct the cost.

Business Insurance: Safety Nets

This isn't your health insurance; this is the stuff that covers your business assets, like that pricey laptop or the irreplaceable manuscript. You can also deduct insurance premiums for liability or property insurance related to your business. If you have decided to go with a Sole Proprietorship, I highly recommend getting some liability insurance, since the corporate structure doesn't protect your personal assets.

Display Materials: Setting the Scene

From tablecloths and banners to book stands and signage, the materials you use to create your display can also be deducted. Think of these as your book's stage props; they set the scene and help tell your story. Even if you're getting crafty with do-it-yourself elements, keep those receipts for the materials you buy.

Over time, your display materials may need some maintenance. Whether it's repairing a banner or upgrading your book stands, these costs are deductible. Keeping your display fresh and up-to-date can make a big difference in attracting potential readers.

Giving to Grow: Charitable Contributions

Sole proprietors can donate to charity, but it must be done as an individual, not through the business.

If, however, you're any of the other structures, such as a Corporation, LLC (more than a single member), or Partnership, you can deduct these contributions, but make sure they're going to qualified organizations. You can't just hand over cash to a friend and call it charity.

Also, if you're donating product, like a book or some character art, you cannot value the donation at the retail price. You must value it at what it cost you, not including your time.

Health Insurance: The Plot Armor

If you're self-employed, you can deduct health insurance premiums. This deduction is usually better taken as a business expense than on the Schedule A, where it can be limited by your income level and whether you have enough in other itemized deductions.

But you can only take the self-employed health insurance deduction if you have a net profit. So, make sure your royalties aren't in the red before you take this deduction. In addition, self-employed authors can only deduct premiums if they don't qualify for employer-subsidized plans, so if you have a day job, do some research first.

If you're a corporate structure, you can deduct health insurance premiums on you and your employees. However, there are a few extra rules around owners' health insurance, so please consult your CPA in this complex matter.

Legal or Professional Services: The Experts

Need a lawyer to look over a publishing contract? How about an accountant to make sense of all these deductions? The fees for these professional services are deductible. If you're setting up an LLC or a Corporation, those costs are also fair game.

Meal and Entertainment Mysteries: What Counts?

For meals, the IRS has decided to get stingy. Business meals are generally deductible at 50%, but they must be directly related to your business activities. This includes meals with potential clients or while traveling for business. Office snacks, coffee, and other meal-related expenses are also 50% deductible.

You can also use a **per diem** rate for meals and incidental expenses when traveling, which can sometimes be more advantageous than deducting actual expenses. Just check the rates for your travel location on the GSA website.

Office Supplies and Rentals: The Essentials

From paper clips to that high-end water cooler you splurged on, office supplies are deductible. Even renting a postage machine or a credit card reader counts. The key is that these are everyday essentials you use in your business operations.

Promotional Items: Freebies and Swag

Bookmarks, posters, postcards, and other promotional items that you hand out at these events can also be deducted as advertising expenses. They're a great way to leave a lasting impression on potential readers. And let's be honest, who doesn't love free stuff?

Rent: Finding Room to Write

If you're renting a studio, office, or even equipment like a high-quality printer, these expenses are deductible. The same goes for renting booths at conventions or market spaces to sell your books.

Repairs and Maintenance: Keeping Things Running

If your trusty computer needs a tune-up, or your printer goes on strike, the costs of repairs and maintenance are deductible. However, if you use the equipment for both business and personal tasks, you should prorate how much you use for each, and only deduct the business-use percentage. For example, if you use your computer 60% for business, you can deduct 60% of the repair costs.

Taxes and Licenses: The Necessary Evils

You can deduct property taxes and business licenses, but not sales tax. Sales tax is more of a pass-through. You collect it and then hand it over to the state. However, if you're paying business property taxes or renewing your business license, those are deductible.

Travel Tales: There and Back Again

Ah, the glamorous life of an author. Jet-setting to conventions, book tours, and speaking engagements. If your travel is primarily for business, you can deduct expenses like transportation, lodging, and meals. But if you're mixing business with pleasure, you'll need to prorate. If you're at a convention and spend 70% of your time on business-related activities, you can deduct 70% of the costs, based on an 8-hour workday. Just remember, your spouse's expenses aren't deductible unless they are also an employee of the business.

If you attend a book fair in New York and spend 70% of your time (based on an 8-hour workday) promoting your book, you can deduct 70% of your travel expenses. Keep those receipts, log your mileage, and be ready to explain your expenses if the IRS decides to play editor.

There are several receipt-scanning apps available to help. A note on how long to keep these paper transactions:

The IRS wants you to keep them for seven years in case they want to conduct an audit. If you don't have the originals, see if you can download transactions from a credit card or bank account. Often, you cannot go back more than a year online, so plan accordingly. And remember if you have anything on thermal paper (faxes) they do fade over time.

In conclusion, understanding what expenses you can deduct is crucial for maximizing your tax return and keeping more of your hard-earned money. Remember, the IRS is like a strict editor. They want to see everything documented and justified. So, keep your records neat and your deductions legitimate, and you'll be on your way to a happy ending with the taxman.

Wage Wishes: Paying Yourself and Others

As a sole proprietor, you can't deduct the wages you pay yourself. Those are considered a return on your investment in the business. However, if you've gone the corporate route (C or S Corporation), you can deduct wages paid to yourself, but you'll also need to report them as income on your personal tax return. It's a bit of a wash, but it's all part of the narrative.

Not Exactly Expenses
Equipment Expedition: Tools of the Trade

For the IRS, equipment isn't just any old pen or sticky note. We're talking about the big-ticket items here, the ones that make your writing life possible and (hopefully) more comfortable. This can include computers, desks, chairs, display equipment, even machinery. Do you use a Cricut to make bookmarks? Do you bind your own books? Have a complex display for book shows? All of these are deductible.

But, of course, the IRS has some rules to follow.

Capitalization Conundrum: When to Depreciate

So, you've splurged on a fancy new laptop that costs more than $1,000 and you plan to use it for the next few years. Congrats! But don't expect to write off that expense all at once. If your shiny new gear is substantial (this is a judgment call based on the size of your business) and lasts longer than a year, you'll need to "capitalize" it.

No, that doesn't mean writing in all caps; it means listing it as an asset and spreading the deduction over its useful life. This process is called depreciation, and it's as fun as it sounds.

For instance, if you bought a $700 booth to display your works at conventions, you can't just slap a $700 deduction on your tax return and call it a day. The IRS says that booth is furniture and the cost should be spread over its life. And as furniture, the IRS says its life is seven years. So, you get to deduct $100 per year, which is like slowly peeling off a Band-Aid.

Depreciation Diaries: Advanced Rules and Methods

The above example is the simplest of methods called, naturally enough, the Straight-Line Method. Divide the total cost by the number of useful years, and expense that even amount each year.

The IRS is fine with Straight-Line for small businesses. However, sometimes it gets stroppy and prefers a more precise method. The reasoning is that, for some equipment, the best use is the early years, and then it gets less efficient. Therefore, the IRS has created several rules like MACRS (Modified Accelerated Cost Recovery

System), Units of Production, or Declining Balance Method.

However, as a small business, these are probably not something you need to bother about.

That being said, there are a couple other tools in the depreciation toolbox. Enter Section 179 depreciation. This magical rule allows you to deduct the full cost of eligible equipment in the year you buy it, but there's a catch. In order to use Section 179 Depreciation, you must be profitable. So, if you're rolling in royalties, go ahead and take that full $700 deduction for your booth in the year of purchase.

There's also something called Bonus Depreciation which lets you deduct a higher percentage of qualifying assets in the year purchased. This varies from year to year and with the type of asset, so this is an area you should consult an expert for the nitty-gritty details. A tax professional can help you navigate this thrilling narrative.

Timing Tactics: Cash vs. Accrual Basis Accounting

Timing and Cash Basis

Timing is everything. Whether you're planning a book launch or deciding when to deduct expenses, the IRS has a particular love for getting things done on time, especially when it comes to recording sales and expenses. This is where the concept of cash basis versus accrual basis accounting comes into play. Most solo authors and small businesses opt for the simpler "cash basis" approach. Here's how it works:

Cash Basis Accounting

Think of this as your "pay as you go" method. If you sell a book in December 2024 but don't get paid until January 2025, you record the sale when you actually receive the payment in January. It's straightforward: money in, sale recorded. Likewise, expenses are recorded when you pay them, not when you incur them.

Accrual Basis Accounting

This is for those who like to keep track of promises and IOUs. If you make a sale in December 2024, you report it as income for 2024, even if you don't see the cash until 2025. You record the expense when you incur it, not necessarily when you pay it. This method is more complex and is typically used by larger companies, but if you like living on the edge, go for it.

The Modified Cash Basis Twist

Now, if you're dealing with inventory, like stacks of your latest novel sitting in your garage, you're in the realm of "modified cash basis." This hybrid approach is often the best fit for Sole Proprietorships, especially when inventory is involved. With modified cash basis, you record income and expenses as they occur, but also consider the cost of goods sold (COGS) and inventory in your accounting. It's like cash basis accounting but with a plot twist.

Why Modified Cash Basis?

Why should you care? Because inventory isn't just sitting there looking pretty. It affects your taxes and your ability to make good decisions. The IRS wants you to match the expense of producing those books (or other products) with the income they generate. So, if you sell a book from your inventory, you record both the sale and the expense of producing that book in the same period.

In terms of decisions, if you bought 300 copies of a book, and sold half of them in one year and the other half in the next year, you don't want the full expense in year one. That's going to skew your profit numbers and make it look like you're losing money. You aren't, because you've still got an investment in those hard copies, ready to sell in year two. It's all about keeping the storyline consistent.

Navigating the labyrinth of business expenses doesn't have to be a thriller or a horror story. Whether you choose cash basis, accrual basis, or modified cash basis accounting, the key is to stay organized and keep good records. Remember, every expense is a potential deduction, and every deduction is a potential plot twist in your financial story.

So, dear author, sharpen your pencils and keep those receipts. Whether it's coffee for that marathon writing session, postage for mailing signed copies, or even that new ergonomic chair to save your back, these are all pieces of the puzzle. And just like writing, the details matter, especially when the tax man comes knocking.

Workbook Exercise and Excel Sheet: Tracking Your Expenses

Exercise: The Expense Tracker
Objective: To create a comprehensive list of expenses for your author business and track them effectively using spreadsheets. This will help you stay organized and ensure you don't miss out on any potential deductions.

Instructions:

List All Possible Expenses: Start by brainstorming all potential expenses related to your author business. These can include:
- Office supplies (pens, notebooks, etc.)
- Equipment (computers, printers, software)
- Book production costs (printing, binding)
- Post Office Box
- Marketing and advertising (business cards, promotional materials)
- Travel expenses (mileage, hotel stays for book events)

- Display costs (booth rentals, display materials for book shows)
- Professional services (editing, cover design, legal fees)
- Memberships and subscriptions (writers' organizations, industry magazines)
- Utilities (internet, phone, electricity for your workspace)

Create an Expense Tracker Sheet: Open a new Excel workbook and create a sheet titled "Expense Tracker."

Set up the following columns:
- Date: When the expense occurred.
- Category: Type of expense (e.g., Office Supplies, Travel, Marketing).
- Description: Brief detail of the expense.
- Amount: The cost of the expense.
- Payment Method: How you paid (credit card, cash, etc.).
- Receipt: Whether you have a receipt (Yes/No).
- Notes: Any additional notes (e.g., "Reimbursed by client").

Monthly Review: Create a separate sheet for each month and label them accordingly (e.g., "August 2024 Expenses"). Transfer your expenses to the appropriate month's sheet, updating the tracker regularly. At the end of each month, total the expenses and review categories to ensure everything is accounted for.

Annual Summary: At the end of the year, create a summary sheet titled "Annual Expense Summary." This sheet should aggregate totals from each month's sheet, categorized by type of expense. This will help you see where your money is going and prepare for tax season.

Example layout:

Category	Total Amount
Office Supplies	$450
Travel	$1,200
Marketing	$600
Professional Services	$800
Display Costs	$300

Review and Adjust: Regularly review your expenses to ensure accuracy. Adjust your categories or tracking methods if needed to better reflect your business needs.

Excel Sheets for Tracking Author Business Expenses

Expense Tracker Template:
- Description: A basic template to record individual expenses with columns for date, category, description, amount, payment method, receipt, and notes.

- Download Example Template

Monthly Expense Tracker:
- Description: Separate sheets for each month, allowing you to track and categorize expenses on a month-by-month basis.
- Download Example Template

Annual Expense Summary:
- Description: An aggregate sheet that sums up expenses from each month and categorizes them, helping you get a big-picture view of your spending.
- Download Example Template

Expense Report Dashboard:
- Description: A more advanced tool with charts and graphs to visualize your spending trends over time.
- Download Example Template

Chapter Six

Your Workspace

Home Office Expenses

Your home office is your sanctuary. It's where the magic happens, where stories come to life, and where your coffee habit may become a tax deduction.

If you're a writer working from home, your cozy nook could be more than just a creative space. It could also unlock valuable tax deductions. Let's explore how your literary lair can become a tax-friendly oasis.

The Basics of Home Office Deductions

Before we get into the nitty-gritty, let's clarify what qualifies as a home office. According to the IRS, your home office must be used *exclusively* and *regularly* for your business. So, if your "writing desk" is also the dining room table used for family dinners, tax deductions won't fly. The space must be dedicated solely to your authorial pursuits. It needs to be where you write, edit, and dream up your next bestseller.

Exclusive Use: The area must be used only for your writing business. That means no Netflix binge-watching or using the space for other purposes. However, that doesn't mean it's the only place you can write. You can still escape to the local coffee shop if your kids are being too loud in the next room.

Regular Use: You need to use the space consistently for your business. Occasional use won't cut it. Regular use doesn't have to be every day (though that would be great). It does need to be more than three or four times a year.

Calculating Your Home Office Space

Let's get into the numbers. Suppose you have a dedicated writing room. Let's call it your "author's haven." If this room is 15x15 feet, that's 225 square feet of space. Now, if your entire house is 2,250 square feet, you're looking at a home office space that takes up 10% of your home. This percentage (225/2250 = 0.10 or 10%) is crucial for calculating your deductible expenses.

Indirect vs. Direct Expenses

Home office deductions fall into two categories: indirect and direct expenses. Let's break them down.

Indirect Expenses: These are costs associated with maintaining your entire home. For instance, mortgage interest, property taxes, utilities, homeowner's insurance, and even rent can be partially deducted. The magic number here is that 10% we calculated earlier. So, if your annual utility bill is $2,000, you can deduct $200 (10%) as a home office expense.

Here's a list of common indirect expenses:

- Mortgage interest
- Property taxes
- Utilities (electricity, water, gas)
- Homeowner's insurance
- Rent
- General home repairs

Remember, only the portion of these expenses that corresponds to your home office space is deductible.

Direct Expenses: These are expenses specifically for your home office. If you have a separate business phone line, buy office furniture, or make repairs in your office, these costs are 100% deductible. So, if the window in your "author's haven" breaks and you replace it for $500, that's a full deduction.

Examples of direct expenses include:

- Office furniture and equipment
- Dedicated phone lines or internet services
- Repairs specific to the office space

Depreciation:

Your home depreciates over time. The IRS allows you to deduct a portion of the depreciation of your home as part of your home office expenses. This deduction is based on the value of your home (excluding the land) and the percentage of your home used for business.

For instance, if your home (excluding land) is valued at $200,000 and you use 10% of it for your writing business, you can depreciate $20,000 over time. The IRS provides tables to calculate the yearly depreciation deduction, which typically spreads over 39 years for commercial property.

The Simplified Option

If calculating the home office deduction seems as complex as the plot of *Inception*, there's a simplified method. The IRS allows a flat rate deduction of $5 per square foot of your home office, up to 300 square feet. So, if your "author's haven" is 225 square feet, you can take a $1,125 deduction (225 sq ft x $5).

This option simplifies the process but may not be as beneficial as the actual expense method, especially if you have high indirect expenses.

The Catch: Profit and Loss

There's a plot twist to all this, though. If your writing business runs at a loss, you can't use home office deductions to deepen that loss. However, don't toss those deductions away like a rejected manuscript. You can carry them forward to future years when your writing royalties come rolling in. Essentially, if you're in the red this year, those deductions can offset future profits.

And one more gotcha in the future. If you have taken depreciation expense on your house, and you later sell your house at a gain, you might have to recapture some of that depreciation expense at the sale. This is another one of those complex areas that it's better to consult a professional for.

Workbook Exercise: List Your Fixed Assets

Now, let's get practical. Take a moment to list out all the fixed assets in your home office. This includes your desk, chair, computer, bookshelves, and any other equipment. Note their purchase dates and costs. This information will be useful not only for your deductions but also for insurance purposes.

Navigating home office deductions may seem like a labyrinth, but with the right guidance, you can emerge victorious, just like a protagonist in a gripping novel. By understanding the rules and keeping good records, you can turn your home office into a tax-efficient creative space. Remember, the IRS's requirements for exclusivity and regularity are your main plot points. Stay within those lines, and your deductions will be as smooth as a well-edited manuscript.

So, whether you're penning the next great novel, a series of captivating short stories, or informative nonfiction, your home office can be a valuable asset, both creatively and financially. Happy writing, and may your deductions be ever in your favor!

Workbook Exercise: Calculate Your Home Office Space

To accurately claim home office deductions, it's essential to determine the percentage of your home used exclusively for your writing business. This exercise will guide you through the process.

Step 1: Measure Your Home Office Space

Identify Your Home Office Area:

• Determine which room or specific area of your home is used solely for your writing business. Remember, this space must be used exclusively for business activities to qualify for deductions.

Measure the Length and Width:

• Using a tape measure, record the length and width of your home office space. If the room has an irregular shape, try to measure it as accurately as possible.
Example:
• Length: 15 feet
• Width: 15 feet

Calculate the Square Footage:

• Multiply the length by the width to find the total square footage of your home office.
• Example calculation: 15 ft (length) X 15 ft (width) = 225 square feet.

Your Calculation:
• Length: _________ feet

- Width: _________ feet
- Total Square Footage of Home Office: _________ sq ft

Step 2: Measure Your Entire Home

Determine the Total Area of Your Home:
- If you don't have the exact square footage of your home, measure each room's length and width, then add them together. Alternatively, consult your home's floor plan or a recent property appraisal.

Example:
- Total Square Footage of Home: 2,250 sq ft

Your Calculation:
- Total Square Footage of Home: _________ sq ft

Step 3: Calculate the Percentage of Your Home Used for Business

Divide the Total Square Footage of Your Home Office by the Total Square Footage of Your Home:

Example Calculation:

$$\frac{225 \text{ sq ft (home office)}}{2250 \text{ sq ft (total home)}} \times 100 = 10\%$$

Your Calculation:

Your Calculation:

$$\frac{\text{Home Office Square Footage}}{\text{Total Home Square Footage}} \times 100$$

Home Office Square Footage×100
- Percentage of Home Used for Business: _________ %

Step 4: Document Your Findings

Record Your Measurements and Calculations:
- Keep a detailed record of your measurements and calculations. This documentation is important for tax purposes and can help if you ever need to provide evidence of your home office setup.

Consider Any Changes:
- If your home office space changes (e.g., you move to a different room or expand your office area), update your measurements and percentage calculation accordingly.

Chapter Seven

Inventory Invasion

Inventory is often shrouded in mystery, a topic seemingly reserved for late-night discussions in dusty accounting offices. However, let's dispel that myth right now.

Inventory, in its simplest form, is the cost of the items you have available for sale. As a writer, artist, or creative entrepreneur, understanding inventory is crucial for managing your business finances and accurately reporting them on your tax return.

Let's break down the concept of inventory and explore what counts as inventory and what doesn't. We'll also demystify how to handle it for tax purposes.

Understanding Inventory: The Basics

Inventory consists of the tangible items you have purchased or created that are intended for sale. This includes finished products, work-in-process items, and materials that will be used to create these products. For instance, if you're an artist, your inventory might include completed paintings, digital prints, matted and bagged prints, or even blank canvases and matboards that will eventually become finished works.

The key factor that differentiates inventory from supplies is traceability. Traceability means you can directly associate an item with a final product. For instance, the cost of a blank canvas can be traced to a specific painting, whereas the cost of a box of pens used for various tasks cannot be tied to any one saleable item.

To include an item in your inventory, you must be able to trace it to a specific piece or product. Let's dive deeper into what that means.

What Counts as Inventory?

• **Finished Products:** These are items ready for sale, such as books, book boxes, bookmarks.

• **Work-in-Process:** These are items that are not yet complete but are in the process of becoming finished products. For example, a partially painted piece of character art

- **Materials:** These are items that will eventually become part of your finished products, such as bookmark blanks or boxes to send your books out in. These items are included in inventory because they can be traced to the final products they will become.

What Doesn't Count as Inventory?

Items that can't be traced to a specific product or are consumed over time fall under "supplies" rather than inventory. Supplies are deductible when purchased and are not tied to the cost of goods sold. Here are some examples:

- **Consumables:** These are items like pens, paints, paper, and other materials that are used up over time. For example, a silver pen for signing books used across multiple author signings cannot be traced to a specific product and is thus considered a supply.

- **Office Supplies:** Items like printer paper (for office use), pens, notepads, and other everyday supplies.

Calculating Inventory: The Year-End Process

To properly account for inventory, you'll need to calculate your inventory at the end of each year. This process involves several key steps:

- **Determine Beginning Inventory:** This is the value of inventory you have on hand at the start of the year. It includes finished products, work-in-process, and materials.

- **Add Purchases:** Throughout the year, you may purchase new materials or create new products. The cost of these additions must be included in your inventory calculation.

- **Subtract Cost of Goods Sold (COGS):** When you sell items, you need to deduct the cost associated with those items from your inventory. Importantly, this is the cost of the items, not the sale price.

- **Determine Ending Inventory:** This is the value of inventory you have on hand at the end of the year. It should match the actual physical count of items you have.

- **Account for Adjustments:** Sometimes, there may be discrepancies between your calculated inventory and the actual inventory on hand. This could be due to damage, theft, or errors. These discrepancies are accounted for as "breakage," "spoilage," "shrinkage," "loss," etc., and can be written off as expenses.

Example Scenario: Calculating Inventory

Let's say you start the year with $120 in inventory, mostly consisting of printed books. During the year, you purchase $800 worth of new books and $200 worth of bookmark blanks, stickers, and packing material for book boxes. You sell $500 worth of these items (at cost).

Here's the calculation:

Beginning Inventory		$120
Add purchases:		
New books	$800	
Materials	$200	
Total Purchases:	$1,000	$1,000
Subtract: Cost of Goods Sold		($500)
Expected Ending Inventory:		$620

At the end of the year, you find you have $500 worth of salable items and $100 in unused books, totaling $600. The difference between the expected inventory ($620) and actual inventory ($600) is $20, accounted for by spoilage or damage (perhaps 50 bookmarks got wet and were damaged, got stolen, or were simply miscounted).

Supplies Surprise: Deducting Materials

While inventory is deducted when sold, supplies are deducted when purchased. Supplies include items like notebooks, pens, pencils, paper, postage supplies, and other consumables. Since these items are used across multiple pieces and cannot be traced to a specific product, they are categorized as expenses rather than inventory.

This distinction is essential because supplies are deductible in the year they are purchased, providing an immediate tax benefit. In contrast, inventory costs are only deductible when the item is sold, which aligns expenses with revenue.

Wage Wars: Handling Wages and Inventory Costs

Another important aspect of managing your creative business is understanding how to handle payroll and related deductions. A sole proprietor cannot deduct their own wages from the business's income. (Corporations can). Instead, any money taken out of the business is considered a withdrawal and is not deductible.

However, if you have employees or contractors, their wages may be deductible, especially if they contribute directly to creating inventory. For instance, if you employ apprentices to help assemble book boxes, their wages can be included in the inventory cost of the items they work on.

This allocation can reduce your taxable income by including a portion of wages in the cost of goods sold. It's essential to keep accurate records of the time spent and tasks performed by employees or contractors that directly contribute to inventory.

Special Considerations for S Corporations

If your business is structured as an S Corporation, there are additional considerations. S Corporation owners must pay themselves a "reasonable salary" before taking profit distributions.

A reasonable salary is defined by the IRS as one that a similar employee would earn for comparable work in the same industry and region.

This salary is subject to payroll taxes, and failure to pay a reasonable salary can result in penalties. Moreover, there is a 20% deduction for qualified business income, but this deduction is only available after deducting reasonable compensation.

In this case, accurately accounting for wages and ensuring compliance with IRS guidelines is crucial. Consult a tax professional to navigate these complexities and optimize your tax situation.

Managing inventory and supplies effectively is a crucial aspect of running a successful creative business. By understanding the differences between inventory and supplies, accurately calculating inventory at year-end, and appropriately accounting for wages, you can ensure compliance with tax regulations and optimize your financial management.

Remember, inventory is a tangible representation of your creative output, while supplies are the tools and materials that fuel your artistic endeavors. By treating these elements with care and precision, you'll not only streamline your business operations but also maximize your tax benefits.

Keep detailed records, stay organized, and don't hesitate to consult with a tax professional to navigate the nuances of inventory management and tax deductions. With these strategies in hand, you'll be well on your way to mastering the financial aspects of your creative business, leaving you free to focus on what you do best. Writing!

Workbook Exercise and Excel Sheet: Valuing Your Inventory

This exercise will help you calculate the value of your inventory at the end of the year. It's essential to accurately determine this value for financial reporting and tax purposes. Follow the steps below and use the provided template to organize your inventory data.

Step 1: List Your Inventory Items

Start by listing all the items in your inventory. Include finished products, work-in-process items, and raw materials that will be used to create finished products.

- **Books**
- **Novellas**
- **Bookmarks**

Write a brief description of each inventory item you have. Be specific enough to distinguish between different types of items.

●

●

●

Step 2: Calculate the Total Inventory Value

Next, figure out how much each item is worth.

● Quantity: Enter the quantity of each item you have on hand.
● Unit Cost: Provide the cost of each unit. This may include materials, labor, and any other direct costs associated with producing the item.
● Multiply the quantity by the unit cost to find the total cost for each item.
● Sum the "Total Cost" column to determine the total value of your inventory. This figure represents the value of all items in your inventory at the end of the year.

Calculation Example:
If you have 50 books at $10 each, 30 novellas at $5 each, and 250 bookmarks valued at $1 each, the total inventory value would be:

Item Description	Quantity	Unit Cost		Total Cost	
Books	50 X $	10	= $		500
Novellas	30 X $	5	= $		150
Bookmarks	250 X $	1	= $		250
Total Inventory Value				$	900

Your inventory:

Item Description	Quantity	Unit Cost	Total Cost
	X	=	
	X	=	
	X	=	
Total Inventory Value			

Step 3: Document and Save Your Inventory Worksheet

Once you have calculated the adjusted inventory value, document all details carefully. This worksheet serves as a crucial record for financial reporting and tax filing. If you're using an Excel sheet, save a copy with the date and clearly label it as your year-end inventory valuation.

Additional Notes:
• Work-in-Process: Include items that are partially completed but have had significant value added to them. Estimate their value based on the stage of completion.

- Raw Materials: Include items that will be used to create finished products, such as blank canvases, frames, or other necessary components.

By following this exercise, you will have a clear and accurate record of your inventory's value. This information is essential for determining your cost of goods sold (COGS) and ensuring accurate financial reporting.

Chapter Eight

Filing Frenzy

Taxes are the perennial anxiety in the story of running a creative business. Just when you're reveling in the joy of crafting your next masterpiece, along comes tax season, demanding your attention like an insistent editor with a red pen. But with a little guidance, you can turn the often-daunting world of taxes into a manageable subplot in your entrepreneurial narrative. Let's embark on a journey through the different taxation structures you might encounter as a writer or creative entrepreneur, starting with income tax basics and delving into specific forms and business entities.

Income Tax Adventures (Federal and State)

No matter where you set your story, the tax collector will always find a way into your plot. In the United States, you're likely to encounter both federal and state income taxes. Federal income tax is a nationwide affair, levied on your earnings by the IRS.

Meanwhile, state income taxes add a local twist, varying by state with different rates and rules. Some states, like Florida and Texas, are plot-free zones for state income tax, while others, like California and New York, have high rates that can feel like a hefty antagonist to your profits.

Mastering Schedule C

For sole proprietors and single-member LLCs, Schedule C is your go-to document for reporting income and expenses from your business. Think of it as your creative project's financial summary.

As an individual, you'll report your income on Form 1040. As a self-employed writer, you'll add this Schedule C to your personal tax return to report business income and expenses.

Here, you'll list all the income you've earned from book sales, freelance gigs, or any other sources. You'll also deduct expenses, such as office supplies, marketing costs, and even that shiny new laptop you bought for drafting your next bestseller. The goal? To arrive at your net profit or loss, which then makes its way to your Form 1040.

Remember, you're also responsible for self-employment taxes, which cover Social Security and Medicare contributions, so factor that into your calculations. When you're an employee, you pay 7.65% in Social Security and Medicare. However, your employer also pays that amount. So, when you're your own employer, you have to pay both sides, for a total of 15.3% on net profits.

Exploring the 1120S

If your creative business has taken on a life of its own and you've structured it as an S Corporation, you'll be filing Form 1120S. This form is where the plot thickens for S Corps, as it reports income, deductions, and credits.

The unique twist with S Corps is the way they handle profits. Instead of the Corporation paying income taxes, the profits (and losses) pass through to the shareholders, who then report them on their personal tax returns. This setup can offer some tax advantages, like avoiding double taxation, but it also comes with the responsibility of paying yourself a reasonable salary as an employee of your own company, a plot point that keeps you compliant with IRS regulations.

Demystifying the 1065

Partnerships, whether it's you and a fellow writer teaming up or a collaboration with other artists, use Form 1065 to report their business's financials. Like an S Corp, a Partnership itself doesn't pay taxes. Instead, the income and deductions pass through to the partners, who report them on their personal returns. The 1065 form is akin to the Partnership's diary, detailing income, expenses, and each partner's share of the profits or losses. This form is complemented by Schedule K-1, which breaks down each partner's share of the business's income and deductions. It's a cooperative venture, both in creativity and in tax responsibility.

That K-1 is then added into your personal tax return, so you're taxed based on that, not at the company level.

Loving the LLC

The LLC is the versatile character actor of the business world. An LLC can be a Sole Proprietorship, a Partnership, or even elect to be taxed as an S Corp or C Corp. The beauty of an LLC lies in its flexibility and the liability protection it offers.

If you're a single-member LLC, you'll likely file taxes using Schedule C, just like a sole proprietor. Basically, the IRS considers it to be what's called a "disregarded entity", which just means it has no legal tax status outside yourself.

But if your LLC has multiple members, it can file as a Partnership using Form 1065 or elect S Corp status and use Form 1120S. The LLC structure allows you to tailor your tax filing to best suit your narrative, providing a blend of simplicity and protection.

Keep in mind that forming an LLC does not automatically change your tax treatment. Unless you elect to be taxed as a corporation, the IRS will continue to treat your LLC as a sole proprietorship or partnership, depending on whether you have multiple members.

Paying Quarterly Estimated Taxes: Except for C Corporations, each of the above structures might require paying taxes every three months, in anticipation of what would be due at year end. This avoids penalties and interest for underpaying when taxes are filed. The goal is to owe less than $1,000 when filing.

The world of taxes may not be the most thrilling chapter in your business story, but understanding the different taxation structures can help you navigate the plot twists with confidence. Whether you're filling out Schedule C as a solo act, exploring the intricacies of Form 1120S as an S

Corp, or partnering up and filing Form 1065, knowing the ins and outs of each form and entity type is crucial.

As with any good story, there's no one-size-fits-all ending. Your unique circumstances will determine the best tax structure for your creative business, so consult with a tax professional to ensure your narrative stays on track. With the right knowledge and preparation, you can keep your financial story a page-turner, leaving you free to focus on the creative chapters ahead.

Chapter Nine

Tax Tales

Sales Tax Shenanigans (State)

Many people ask how Sales Tax comes into play with income. In reality, we never 'earn' sales tax. We merely collect it and hold it for the state government. Whenever we make a sale that is taxable, we collect the sales tax.

Once a month, or once a quarter, or sometimes once a year, we tally up all the sales tax we *should* have collected and pay it to the state. That *should* is a very important word! If you did not collect sales tax, but should have, you're *still* liable to pay it to the state, out of your own pocket.

Also, the sales tax is defined by where you're conducting business in most states. For a physical sale transaction, if I sell a book at an author signing in Florida, I charge Florida sales tax. If the sale is across state lines, Florida law says

I don't have to charge sales tax for physical sales, but the other state wants their cut. If I move my place of business – like setting up a booth in Georgia – I charge and pay Georgia sales tax. Some states (like Georgia) have a one-time special event tax form so I don't have to register for a standing account. Some don't, so you will need to check each and every state you physically sell in.

Since Sales Tax is not income, when we collect sales tax we don't include that as income on our tax return, so it isn't subject to income tax. Paying sales tax isn't an expense that we can deduct, either. It doesn't go on the income tax return at all. See resources later in this chapter.

The Sales Tax Treasure Map

Collecting sales tax can feel like navigating a treasure map, with state and local governments waiting at every turn to claim their share of the booty.

Here's how to chart your course:

Know Your Rates: Each state, and sometimes even individual counties or cities, can have different sales tax rates. It's essential to research and apply the correct rate for your location.

Track Your Sales: Keep meticulous records of all your sales, noting where each customer is located. This helps you determine how much tax you should be collecting.

Register When Needed: If you move or set up shop in a different state or county, make sure to register for a sales tax permit in that location. Some areas have streamlined processes for short-term events, so always check the local requirements.

Watch your deadlines: Some states require monthly filing, while others might allow quarterly or annual, depending on your total sales. Deadlines vary by state, so keep them on your calendar.

Collecting the Bounty: Sales Tax Obligations

Once you've collected the treasure (sales tax), it's time to ensure it gets to its rightful owner (the state government):

- **Regular Remittance:** Depending on your state's requirements, remit collected sales tax monthly, quarterly, or annually. Missing these deadlines can lead to penalties and interest.
- **Accurate Reporting:** When you file your sales tax returns, report accurately. Discrepancies can trigger audits, leading to more headaches.

- **Stay Informed:** Tax laws change frequently. Keep up with any changes in your state's sales tax laws to avoid unintentional non-compliance.
- **Seek Help When Needed:** If the process becomes overwhelming, don't hesitate to seek professional help. A good accountant or tax advisor can help navigate the complex waters of sales tax compliance.

The South Dakota Switch: Sales Tax Changes

In 2018, the Supreme Court decision in South Dakota v. Wayfair, Inc. shook up the sales tax landscape for online sellers. Here's the scoop:

- **Old Rule:** Under the Quill Corp v. North Dakota ruling, interstate online sales were exempt from sales tax if the seller had no physical presence (nexus) in the buyer's state.
- **New Rule:** The Wayfair decision overturned this, allowing states to require online sellers to collect and remit sales tax, even without physical presence.

What This Means for You

- **Understanding sales tax nexus:** If you have a physical presence of sales in a state, you most likely have a nexus, such as selling at a book fair. Your home state is always a nexus. But if you make enough sales in another state, it may create a nexus. Most have a minimum number or amount of sales.

- **Exemptions:** South Dakota has set exemptions for small businesses with fewer than 200 customers or less than $100,000 in sales in the state. Other states might have different thresholds or none at all.

- **Research Required:** Selling to customers in different states means researching and complying with each state's sales tax laws. This includes determining if sales tax is due, registering for a sales tax permit, and collecting and remitting the tax. See the Resources section for some links that can help you stay abreast of changes. If you're using a platform like Etsy or Amazon, they should be collecting and paying sales tax for you. Research to ensure that whatever sale platform you use has this covered.

- **Increased Burden:** This decision places a significant burden on small businesses. The time and effort required to ensure compliance can be substantial, potentially impacting your ability to focus on other aspects of your business.

Property Tax Puzzles (County)

Property taxes can feel like a mystery novel, but we'll help you crack the case. Property tax is usually based on the value of property you own, like your home or office. If you rent, or if you don't use a home office, this type of tax might not apply to you.

- **Valuation Whodunit:** Your property's assessed value is determined by your local county assessor. They use various methods, sometimes involving a magnifying glass and a deerstalker hat (okay, maybe not literally), to determine how much your property is worth.
- **Rate Riddle:** Once your property's value is set, it's multiplied by the local tax rate. This rate can vary widely from one county to another, so it's worth researching your area's rates.
- **Deduction Detective:** Some property taxes can be deducted on your federal income tax return if you itemize deductions. You can also prorate your property taxes on your home office deductions.

Business Tax/License Fees (Local)

Running a business isn't just about writing; it's also about navigating the labyrinth of local business taxes and license fees.

- **Permit Prowess:** Most local governments require businesses to obtain a business license. This usually involves paying a fee, which can vary based on your business type and size. Think of it as your entry ticket to the entrepreneurial stage.
- **Fee Frolics:** In addition to the initial license fee, some locations charge annual renewal fees or additional taxes

based on your business revenue. It's a bit like paying rent on your literary café, but to the city.

• **Zoning Zingers:** Ensure your business location complies with local zoning laws. Nothing ruins a good plot like finding out your cozy writing nook isn't zoned for business use.

Self-Employment Taxes: Twice the Pain

When you're self-employed, you're both the employer and the employee, which means double the tax fun.

• **Double Trouble:** As a self-employed individual, you pay both the employee and employer portions of Social Security and Medicare taxes. This can feel like being the protagonist and the antagonist in your own tax story. If you work for someone else, you pay half (7.65% for Social Security and Medicare) and they pay the other half.

However, if you're your own employer, you get the lovely thrill of paying both halves yourself, 15.3%. Keep in mind that this tax is only on net profits, not gross income.

• **Quarterly Quirks:** To avoid penalties, you need to make estimated tax payments quarterly. It's like writing four mini-novels throughout the year instead of one epic tome. The goal is not to have to owe more than $1,000 on your personal federal income tax return when you file next year. Any more than that and you may accrue underpayment penalties and interest.

- **Deduction Drama:** You can deduct the employer portion of your self-employment taxes when calculating your adjusted gross income. It's not a happy ending, but at least it's a subplot that works in your favor.

Workbook Exercise: List your Tax Obligations

Exercise Instructions: Understanding your tax obligations is crucial for managing your small writing business. Use this exercise to identify and list all the taxes you may need to pay. Take a few moments to think about each category and write down your specific obligations.

Income Tax:

- Federal Income Tax
- State Income Tax
- Local Income Tax (if applicable)

Sales Tax:
- State Sales Tax
- Local Sales Tax

- Sales Tax Permits/Registrations

Property Tax:
- Property Tax on Business Location
- Personal Property Tax on Business Equipment (if applicable)

Self-Employment Tax:
- Social Security Tax
- Medicare Tax
- Quarterly Estimated Payments

Business Tax/License Fees:
- Business License Fee
- Renewal Fees
- Zoning Fees (if applicable)

Employment Tax (if you have employees):
- Federal Employment Tax
- State Employment Tax
- Unemployment Tax

Other Taxes/Fees:
- Special Local Taxes or Fees
- Industry-Specific Taxes or Fees

Reflective Questions:
- Which of these taxes were you already aware of?

• Are there any new tax obligations you discovered through this exercise?

• What steps can you take to ensure you stay compliant with all your tax obligations?

• Do you need to seek professional help for any of these tax categories?

Action Plan:

• Research: Spend some time researching any tax obligations you're not familiar with.

• Organize: Create a calendar or system to keep track of tax due dates and payment schedules.

• Consult: Consider consulting with a tax professional to ensure you're compliant with all local, state, and federal tax laws.

Note: This list may not cover all possible taxes depending on your specific business situation and location. Always check with a tax professional for comprehensive guidance tailored to your business.

Chapter Ten

Formidable Forms

Navigating through the forest of tax forms out there can feel like you're flipping through an encyclopedia of bureaucratic jargon, but with a few simple tools, you can find your way down the correct path. More information and step-by-step instructions to all these forms can be found on www.irs.gov/forms.

Going Solo: Sole Proprietorship Tax Forms
• Form 1040: This is your main character. As a self-employed writer, you'll use this form to report your personal income.
• Schedule C: You'll detail your business income and expenses here.
• Schedule SE: This form helps you calculate your self-employment taxes.

- Form 1099-NEC: If you hire freelancers, you'll need to send them this form to report payments made for their services.
- Form 8829: If you have a home office, this form allows you to deduct those expenses.

S Corp/C Corp: The Corporate Chronicles

- Form 1120 (C Corp): This is the primary form for C Corporations, used to report the Corporation's income, gains, losses, deductions, and credits.
- Form 1120S (S Corp): For S Corporations, this form takes center stage, reporting the income, deductions, and other financial details.
- Schedule K-1 (Form 1120S): Each shareholder receives this form to report their share of the Corporation's income, deductions, and credits on their personal tax return.
- Form 941: This form is for quarterly federal tax returns, reporting income taxes, Social Security, and Medicare taxes withheld from employees' paychecks.
- Form 940: Used for annual federal unemployment (FUTA) tax returns.
- Form 1099-NEC: If your Corporation hires independent contractors, you'll need to send them this form to report payments made.

Partnerships: The Collaborative Plot

- Form 1065: This is your Partnership's main form, used to report the business's income, deductions, gains, losses, etc.
- Schedule K-1 (Form 1065): Each partner gets this form to report their share of the Partnership's income, deductions, and credits on their personal tax return.
- Form 941: For reporting quarterly federal tax returns, including income, Social Security, and Medicare taxes withheld from employees' paychecks.
- Form 940: Used for annual federal unemployment (FUTA) tax returns.
- Form 1099-NEC: If the Partnership hires freelancers, you'll need to send them this form to report payments made for their services.

LLCs: The Versatile Tale

- Form 1040 (Single-Member LLC): As a single-member LLC, you'll use this form to report your personal income.
- Schedule C (Single-Member LLC): Detail your business income and expenses here.
- Form 1065 (Multi-Member LLC): For multi-member LLCs, use this form to report the business's income, deductions, gains, losses, etc.
- Schedule K-1 (Form 1065): Each member receives this form to report their share of the LLC's income, deductions, and credits on their personal tax return.

- Form 8832: This form is used to elect the classification of your LLC for federal tax purposes (as a Corporation, Partnership, or disregarded entity).
- Form 941: For reporting quarterly federal tax returns, including income, Social Security, and Medicare taxes withheld from employees' paychecks.
- Form 940: Used for annual federal unemployment (FUTA) tax returns.
- Form 1099-NEC: If your LLC hires freelancers, you'll need to send them this form to report payments made.

Deadline Drama: Staying on Schedule

Deadlines aren't just for manuscripts; the IRS has its own deadlines that demand your attention. Remember this: if you file an extension, that is not an extension of any taxes due, just filing the forms. If you believe you will owe taxes, make that payment before the original due date to avoid penalties and interest.

- March 15th: If you've got a Partnership or an S corporate structure, this is the deadline for your return. You can file for an extension to October 15th.
- April 15th: The big one! Your personal federal income tax return is due. Mark it on your calendar with a red pen. You can file for an extension to October 15th.
- April 15th: Yes, again. This is the deadline to file 1120 for C Corporations. You can file for an extension to October 15th.

- June 15th, September 15th, January 15th: These dates are crucial for quarterly estimated tax payments. Missing them can lead to penalties, and nobody wants a plot twist like that.
- January 31st: If you've hired freelancers, make sure to send out 1099-NEC forms by this date. This is also when any W-2s are due, if you have employees.

Estimated Taxes and Quarterly Payments: Avoiding Surprises

Nobody likes surprises, especially from the IRS. To keep your story on track, make those estimated tax payments quarterly.

- Estimate Your Income: Look at your previous year's income and project what you expect to earn this year.
- Divide and Conquer: Split your estimated taxes into four payments. This way, you're not hit with a massive bill at the end of the year.
- Use Form 1040-ES: This form will help you calculate and make your estimated tax payments.

Common Tax Mistakes and How to Avoid Them

Even seasoned writers can fall into common tax traps. Here's how to avoid turning your financial story into a tragedy:

- Mixing Personal and Business Expenses: Keep these separate. Always use a separate bank account and credit card exclusively for your writing business.
- Forgetting to Deduct Business Expenses: Office supplies, software, and even research trips can be deductible.
- Not Keeping Receipts: Keep all your receipts. They're your proof of expenses and can save you during an audit.

Audit Adventures: Preparing for the Unexpected

Audits can feel like an unexpected plot twist, but with some preparation, you can handle them like a pro.

- Keep Detailed Records: Maintain records of all income, expenses, and receipts. Good documentation is your best defense.
- Know Your Rights: If you're audited, understand your rights. You can have representation and appeal decisions.
- Stay Calm: Audits are stressful, but staying organized and calm can help you navigate the process smoothly.

Tax Tools: Software and Services

In the digital age, tax tools are the trusty sidekicks every author needs. Here are some that can make your tax journey easier:

- QuickBooks Self-Employed: This software helps track your income, expenses, and mileage. It also simplifies quarterly tax payments.
- TurboTax Self-Employed: A popular choice for filing your taxes, it guides you through the process and helps find deductions.
- TaxJar: Perfect for those who sell books online, it automates sales tax calculations and filings.
- TaxAct: Another tax filing option, it also guides you through with a detailed questionnaire.

Workbook Exercise: Listing Your Tax Forms

Let's make sure you're prepared for the next tax season. Use this exercise to list all the tax forms you need for your writing business.

Exercise Instructions:

- Identify Your Forms: Based on the sections above, list out the forms you need.
- Gather Your Forms: Find and download these forms from the IRS website.
- Create a Filing System: Set up a system (digital or physical) to keep these forms organized.

Forms to List:
- Form 1040
- Schedule C

- Schedule SE
- Form 1099-NEC
- Form 8829
- Form 1040-ES

Reflective Questions:

- Do you have all the forms you need for your writing business?
- Are there any forms you're unfamiliar with and need to research?
- How can you better organize your tax forms to ensure a smooth filing process?

Action Plan:

- Research: Spend time understanding each form and its requirements.
- Organize: Create a filing system for easy access and reference.
- Consult: If needed, consult with a tax professional to ensure you're on the right track.

Chapter Eleven

Advanced Tax Strategies

Plotting Profit: Tax Planning for Authors

As authors, we get a thrill seeing our book climb the charts, the joy of fan mail, and the sweet sound of royalties hitting our bank account. But with great profit comes great responsibility, especially when it comes to taxes.

Just as every story needs a plot, your financial life as an author needs careful planning to ensure your profits don't get swallowed up by taxes.

Tax planning isn't just for the corporate bigwigs; it's crucial for authors too. Whether you're self-publishing or traditionally published, having a tax strategy in place can help you keep more of your hard-earned money.

Think of it like plotting your story arc. Each decision you make should guide you toward a satisfying conclusion where your financial story ends happily ever after. Unlike a dramatic fiction plot, tax planning doesn't need unexpected twists to work in your favor.

One of the first steps in tax planning is understanding your income sources. As an author, your income might come from advances, royalties, speaking engagements, or even merchandise sales. Each of these has its own tax implications, so it's important to keep track of where your money is coming from. You wouldn't want to miss a plot twist in your novel, and you definitely don't want to miss reporting a source of income to the IRS.

Next, consider your expenses. The saying "you have to spend money to make money" often rings true. Expenses like research materials, writing software, promotional costs, and even trips to that cozy café where you wrote half your book can be deducted from your income, reducing your overall tax liability. Keeping track of these expenses throughout the year is one plot point you don't want to overlook.

But tax planning isn't just about tracking income and expenses. It's also about timing. For example, if you anticipate a particularly profitable year, you might want to accelerate certain expenses, like buying that new laptop or attending a writing conference. That way, you can deduct them in the current tax year. Alternatively, if you expect a lower income year, you might delay some expenses to maximize deductions in the following year. It's like pacing your story. Sometimes you speed up, sometimes you slow down, all to keep your narrative flowing smoothly. Except instead of narrative flow, it's profit flow.

Another advanced strategy is to consider the structure of your writing business. Are you operating as a sole proprietor, or would it make sense to establish an LLC or even a Corporation? Each structure has different tax implications, and the right choice can help you minimize taxes and protect your personal assets. Just like deciding whether your protagonist should go it alone or assemble a team, choosing the right business structure can have a big impact on your success.

Also, don't forget about retirement planning. As an author, you're your own boss, which means you're also responsible for your own retirement savings. Contributing to a retirement account not only helps secure your future but can also provide tax benefits today. It's like writing the sequel before you've finished the first book. You're setting yourself up for success down the line. I highly recommend speaking with a financial planner to ensure you have some retirement funds.

Year-Round Tax Strategies: Staying Ahead

Taxes aren't just a once-a-year affair. They're a year-round responsibility. Just like you wouldn't wait until the last minute to write your novel, you shouldn't wait until tax season to start thinking about your taxes. Staying ahead of the game with year-round tax strategies can save you time, money, and a lot of stress when April 15th rolls around.

One of the most important year-round strategies is estimated tax payments. As a self-employed author, you're responsible for paying taxes on your income throughout the year, not just at the end of it. This means making quarterly estimated tax payments to the IRS. It's like delivering chapters to your editor in chunks. Breaking it down makes the whole process more manageable and ensures you don't have a massive tax bill to deal with at the end of the year.

To calculate your estimated taxes, start by looking at your income and expenses from the previous year. This will give you a baseline for what to expect in the current year. Don't forget to factor in any changes, like a new book deal or increased marketing expenses, that might affect your income or deductions. The key is to stay flexible and adjust your payments as needed throughout the year. After all, every good plot has its twists and turns, and your income might too.

Another year-round strategy is to stay on top of your deductions. Throughout the year, you'll likely incur a variety of business expenses, from office supplies to travel costs. Keeping detailed records of these expenses as they occur will make your life much easier when it's time to file your taxes. Plus, it ensures you don't miss out on any deductions you're entitled to. It's like keeping track of your subplots. Staying organized helps you tie everything together in the end.

Speaking of deductions, don't forget about the home office deduction (see Chapter Five). If you have a dedicated space in your home where you do the majority of your writing, you may be able to deduct a portion of your rent or mortgage, utilities, and other home-related expenses. Ensure your home office meets the IRS requirements. It needs to be used regularly and exclusively for your writing business.

Reducing Tax Liability: Strategies and Tips

No one wants to pay more taxes than they have to. The good news is, with a little bit of planning and some savvy strategies, you can reduce your tax liability and keep more money in your pocket. It's similar to trimming the fat from your manuscript; cutting out unnecessary tax payments makes for a much cleaner financial story.

One of the most effective ways to reduce your tax liability is to maximize your deductions. As we've discussed, keeping track of your business expenses is crucial. But it's not just about tracking the obvious costs like office supplies or travel. Look for less obvious deductions, like the cost of professional development courses, books and magazines related to your writing, or even a portion of your phone bill if you use your phone for business purposes.

Another strategy is to take advantage of tax credits. Unlike deductions, which reduce your taxable income, tax credits reduce your actual tax bill dollar for dollar. As an author, you might be eligible for credits like the Lifetime Learning Credit if you're taking courses to improve your craft, or the Savers Credit if you're contributing to a retirement account. Tax credits can be a bit harder to come by, but they're worth the effort. This might be an area to call on a professional. These credits change from year to year, and tax professionals keep track of updates.

If you have employees or pay contractors, like an editor or graphic designer, you may be able to claim additional deductions for wages, benefits, and even certain payroll taxes. Make sure you're following the IRS guidelines for classifying workers, as misclassification can lead to penalties.

Speaking of employees, don't forget about retirement plans. If you set up a retirement plan for yourself (and any employees), contributions to the plan can be deducted from your taxable income. This not only reduces your current tax liability but also helps you save for the future. Plus, the IRS offers tax credits to small businesses (including self-employed individuals) that set up new retirement plans. Planning now can pay off big in the future.

Finally, consider deferring income to reduce your tax liability. If you expect to be in a lower tax bracket next year, you might delay receiving income until then. This can be done by postponing the release of a new book or negotiating with your publisher to receive royalties after the start of the new tax year. You might also buy new equipment in December, to capture the depreciation expense in the old year, rather than in January. Timing is everything.

Record-keeping and Documentation: Best Practices

Keeping records probably isn't your favorite part of being an author. But just like keeping track of your characters, setting, and plot points is essential to writing a coherent story, maintaining accurate financial records is key to managing your taxes effectively. And, just as with writing, a little organization can save you a lot of headaches down the road.

The first rule of record-keeping is to be thorough. You'll want to keep track of all your income and expenses related to your writing business. This includes not just the obvious things like royalties and book advances, but also any side income from speaking engagements, workshops, or freelance writing. On the expense side, make sure you're recording everything from office supplies to travel costs, and even that fancy coffee you buy to fuel your writing sessions.

One of the best ways to stay organized is to separate your business and personal finances. If you haven't already, consider opening a separate bank account and credit card for your writing business. This makes it much easier to track your income and expenses and ensures you don't miss any deductions.

Workbook Exercise: Reducing Next Year's Taxes

Part 1: Reflect on This Year's Taxes

Review Your Income Sources:
• List all the sources of income you had this year (e.g., book royalties, advances, speaking fees, freelance writing, merchandise sales).
• Were there any income sources you hadn't anticipated?
• Did you find it easy or challenging to track your income throughout the year?

Assess Your Deductions:
• List the business expenses you deducted this year (e.g., office supplies, software, professional development, travel).
• Did you discover any deductions you weren't aware of before?
• Were there any expenses you forgot to track or weren't sure if they were deductible?

Estimate Your Tax Liability:

• How did your tax liability compare to what you expected?

• If you made estimated tax payments, were they sufficient, or did you end up owing more than anticipated?

Part 2: Identify Potential Deductions and Credits for Next Year

List New Income Sources Expected Next Year:

• Do you anticipate any new sources of income next year (e.g., a new book release, a larger advance, new freelance clients)?

• How might these affect your tax liability?

Explore Additional Deductions:

• Are there any new business expenses you expect to incur next year (e.g., purchasing new writing equipment, attending a conference, hiring an editor)?

• Consider less obvious expenses you might be able to deduct, such as a portion of your internet bill, the cost of books or research materials, or subscription services for writing tools.

• Make a list of potential deductions to track more closely next year.

Research Applicable Tax Credits:

- Are you planning to take any courses, workshops, or training that might qualify for the Lifetime Learning Credit?
- Are you contributing to a retirement account, and if so, could you qualify for the Saver's Credit?
- Note any tax credits that might apply to your situation next year.

Part 3: Develop a Tax Strategy

Plan Your Expenses:
- Are there any expenses you can accelerate into the current year to maximize your deductions?
- Conversely, are there any expenses you can delay until next year if you expect your income to be higher?

Consider Your Business Structure:
- Is your current business structure (Sole Proprietorship, LLC, Corporation) still the best fit for your situation?
- If you haven't yet formed a business entity, would it make sense to do so?

Estimate Next Year's Taxes:
- Based on your expected income and deductions, estimate your tax liability for next year.
- Will you need to adjust your quarterly estimated tax payments to avoid a large tax bill at the end of the year?

Set Up a Record-keeping System:

- Review your current record-keeping practices. Are they working for you, or do you need to make changes?
- Consider using a digital tool or app to help you track income and expenses more easily.
- If you don't already have separate accounts for your writing business, make a plan to set them up.

Part 4: Create an Action Plan

Prioritize Your Tasks:

- List the top three actions you'll take to reduce your tax liability next year (e.g., setting up a new retirement account, adjusting your estimated tax payments, researching a new tax credit).

Set Deadlines:

- Assign deadlines to each of your top three actions to ensure you stay on track.

Monitor Your Progress:

- Schedule a mid-year check-in to review your income, expenses, and tax liability. Adjust your plan as needed.

Celebrate Your Wins:

- Recognize the steps you've taken to reduce your tax burden, and celebrate your progress, whether that's with a small treat or a well-deserved break.

Chapter Twelve

International Intrigue

The Global Gain: Managing International Sales

There's something thrilling about knowing that your stories are being enjoyed by readers in Tokyo, Paris, or Sydney.

Before you start dreaming of globe-trotting royalties, there's an important international twist to consider: taxes. Understanding these issues upfront can help you avoid unpleasant surprises and keep your profits intact.

When your books start selling internationally, the financial landscape shifts, and it's crucial to understand how to manage these global gains. Whether you're selling through an online platform like Amazon or distributing through international publishers, knowing the tax implications can keep your profits from disappearing into the vast expanse of international regulations.

Understanding the Basics of International Sales

When you sell your books to readers in other countries, you're earning income in those countries. This opens up a whole new chapter in your tax story. Depending on where your readers are, you might need to pay taxes not just in your home country but also in the countries where your books are sold.

If you're selling through a major online retailer, the platform may automatically handle some of the tax requirements for you. For example, Amazon might collect and remit Value Added Tax (VAT) on your behalf for sales in certain countries. However, this doesn't mean you're off the hook entirely. You'll still need to report this income on your tax return, and depending on your home country's tax laws, you may need to pay additional taxes.

Withholding Taxes: The International Twist

One of the key concepts to understand with international sales is withholding tax. Some countries require a portion of the income you earn from sales in that country to be withheld and paid directly to their government.

For instance, if you sell books in Canada, 15% of your royalties may be withheld, but the rate could be higher or lower depending on any tax treaties in place. This amount is then paid to the Canadian tax authorities, and you receive the rest. The tricky part is that you may still have to report this income and the withholding on your tax return in your home country.

The Role of Double Taxation

Double taxation might sound like the villain of our tax tale, but it's a real issue for authors with international sales. This occurs when you're taxed on the same income in two different countries. For instance, you could end up paying taxes on your royalties in both the country where the book was sold and in your home country. Fortunately, there are ways to prevent this from turning your profits into a sob story, which we'll cover in the next section on tax treaties.

Suppose you're an author based in the U.S. with book sales in Germany. Germany withholds 10% of your royalties for taxes, and then the U.S. also taxes this income. Without proper planning or understanding of tax treaties, you could effectively pay 25-30% of your income in taxes.

To manage your international sales effectively, it's important to keep detailed records of where your books are being sold and how much income you're earning from each country.

The Currency Conundrum: Handling Different Currencies

You've written the book, you've cracked the international market, and now you're seeing payments come in from around the world. But the numbers don't quite add up. Your royalties seem to be dancing to a different tune, and that's thanks to the currency conundrum.

When you start dealing with international sales, you're likely to receive payments in multiple currencies. While it might feel a bit glamorous to see euros, pounds, or yen hitting your account, it also adds a layer of complexity to your financial management. Let's unravel this mystery together.

Understanding Exchange Rates

The first thing to know is that exchange rates are the rules of this currency game. Exchange rates determine how much one currency is worth compared to another. These rates fluctuate daily based on various factors like economic conditions, interest rates, and global market trends.

For example, if you're selling books in the UK, your royalties might be paid in British pounds. But when those pounds are converted to your home currency, the amount you actually receive can vary depending on the exchange rate at the time of conversion. It's a bit like translating your novel into another language. Sometimes the meaning (or in this case, the money) doesn't translate perfectly.

The Impact of Currency Fluctuations

Currency fluctuations can be both a blessing and a curse. On a good day, a favorable exchange rate might boost your income, giving you more in your home currency than you expected. On a bad day, an unfavorable exchange rate could shrink your earnings, leaving you with less than anticipated.

For example, let's say you're based in the US and you receive royalties from a European publisher in euros. If the euro strengthens against the dollar, you'll get more dollars for each euro. But if the euro weakens, you'll end up with fewer dollars.

Strategies for Managing Currency Risk

While you can't control exchange rates, there are ways to manage the risks associated with currency fluctuations:

Consider Currency Hedging:

• Some authors working with large sums may consider hedging, which is a financial strategy used to lock in a specific exchange rate. This can protect you from adverse currency movements, but it's more advanced and may not be necessary for everyone.

For example, you can arrange with your bank to lock in a rate for converting a portion of your royalties, which helps protect against sharp declines in currency value.

Use Multi-Currency Accounts:

• If you frequently receive payments in different currencies, consider opening a multi-currency bank account. This allows you to hold different currencies in their original form, giving you the flexibility to exchange them when the rates are more favorable.

Plan for Exchange Rate Changes:
• Keep an eye on economic trends that might affect exchange rates. For instance, major political events, changes in interest rates, or economic instability in a particular region can all impact currency values.
• If you're planning a major financial move, like reinvesting your royalties or making a large purchase,

try to time it when exchange rates are in your favor.

Include Currency Fluctuations in Your Budget:
• When budgeting for the year, factor in potential currency fluctuations. This can help you avoid surprises and better manage your cash flow.
• Consider working with a financial advisor who understands international markets. They can provide insights into currency trends and help you develop a strategy to maximize your earnings.

Pay Attention to Fees:
• Be aware that banks and payment processors often charge fees for currency conversion. These fees can eat into your profits, so it's important to understand how much you're being charged and look for ways to minimize these costs.

Example: Tracking Currency Impact

Let's say you receive $1,000 in royalties from a UK publisher. You would receive approximately £769.23 when converted at an exchange rate of 1.30 USD per GBP. However, if the exchange rate changes to 1 GBP = 1.25 USD by the time you exchange it, your payment would drop to about $961.54.

That's a $38.46 difference simply due to exchange rate fluctuations! By keeping track of these changes and being strategic about when you convert your money, you can minimize the impact on your earnings.

Tax Treaties: Navigating International Agreements

When you earn income in another country, you'll want to find out if the US has a tax treaty with that country. Imagine tax treaties as peace agreements between countries, designed to ensure that you don't get taxed twice on the same income. These treaties are essential tools for authors navigating the complex world of international sales.

I want to emphasize, before we get too deep in the weeds about tax treaties, that this is a complex and specialized area even for those with accounting degrees. Don't feel bad about seeking expert help.

Understanding Tax Treaties

A tax treaty is an agreement between two countries that outlines how income earned in one country will be taxed in the other. The goal is to prevent double taxation, where you'd have to pay taxes on the same income in both countries. Tax treaties also clarify which country has the right to tax certain types of income, like royalties, and can reduce the amount of withholding tax taken from your international earnings.

For example, if you're a U.S.-based author and you sell books in Germany, a tax treaty between the U.S. and Germany might reduce or eliminate the withholding tax that Germany would otherwise take from your royalties. This means more money in your pocket and less stress come tax time.

Researching Applicable Tax Treaties

Before we go any further, let me say that tax treaties are complex and written in bureaucratic language mixed with tax law. They are not easy to read, even for a trained accountant. This is absolutely an area where asking for professional help is advised.

However, if you really want to delve into this yourself, the first step in navigating tax treaties is to find out if your home country has a treaty with the countries where your books are sold. Many countries, like the U.S., Canada, and the UK, have tax treaties with a wide range of nations. You can typically find these treaties on your government's tax agency website or by consulting a tax professional who specializes in international taxation.

When reviewing a tax treaty, pay attention to the sections that discuss royalties and withholding taxes. These sections will outline the specific tax rates that apply to your income and how to claim any benefits provided by the treaty.

Filing for Treaty Benefits

To take advantage of the benefits provided by a tax treaty, you'll often need to file specific forms or documentation with the tax authorities in the country where your income is earned. For example, if you're claiming reduced withholding tax on royalties under a treaty, you might need to submit a form to the foreign tax authority, such as the IRS Form W-8BEN for U.S. authors.

Filing for treaty benefits can be a bit like navigating a labyrinth, but it's worth the effort. By properly claiming these benefits, you can significantly reduce the amount of tax withheld from your international royalties and avoid double taxation.

Example: Applying a Tax Treaty

Let's say you're an author based in the UK, and you've started selling books in Japan. Without a tax treaty, Japan might withhold 20% of your royalties as tax. However, thanks to a tax treaty between the UK and Japan, you may be able to reduce this withholding to 10% or even 0%, depending on the specifics of the treaty.

To claim this benefit, you'd need to file the appropriate forms with the Japanese tax authorities, providing proof of your UK residency and any other required information. Once your application is approved, the reduced withholding rate would apply, meaning more of your royalties make their way back to you.

Strategizing with Tax Treaties

Here are a few strategies to help you navigate tax treaties effectively.

Research applicable treaties:

• Check if there's a tax treaty between your home country and the sales country. Identify the relevant sections concerning royalties and withholding tax rates.

Consult with an International Tax Expert:

• If you're earning significant income from international sales, it's worth consulting with a tax professional who understands international tax treaties. They can help you identify applicable treaties and ensure you're taking full advantage of them.

Keep Accurate Records:
• As with all things tax-related, documentation is key. Keep detailed records of your international income, including where it was earned and how much tax was withheld. This will be crucial when filing for treaty benefits and preparing your tax return.

Understand Residency Rules:
• Tax treaties often depend on your residency status, so it's important to understand the rules around residency in your home country and the countries where you earn income. If you're considered a resident of multiple countries, this can complicate things, so seek professional advice if needed.

Plan for Treaty Applications:
• Some treaty benefits require advance application, so don't wait until the last minute. Plan ahead and file any necessary forms well before your tax deadlines.

By understanding and leveraging tax treaties, you can keep more of your hard-earned international income, ensuring that your writing journey continues to be as profitable as it is adventurous.

As you venture into the world of international book sales, remember that managing these global gains requires a bit of extra effort and knowledge. But with the right strategies, you can navigate currency fluctuations, minimize withholding taxes, and take full advantage of tax treaties. So, go forth and let your stories reach readers around the globe, knowing that you're well-prepared to handle the international intrigue of taxes.

Chapter Thirteen

Future Forecasting

Future Changes in Tax Laws

Tax laws can change unexpectedly, like plot twists in a novel. But with a bit of planning, you can stay ahead of these changes and keep your finances as successful as your writing.

In this section, we'll explore how to anticipate and adapt to future changes in tax laws, so you're never caught off guard.

Keeping an Eye on the Horizon

The world of taxes is constantly evolving. Governments regularly update tax codes to reflect economic shifts, political priorities, and new societal needs. These changes can range from minor adjustments to major overhauls that significantly impact how much you owe, what you can deduct, and how you plan for the future.

To stay informed, consider the following strategies:

Stay Updated on Legislative Changes:

• Subscribe to tax updates from sites like the IRS Newsroom, Tax Foundation, or accounting blogs such as The Balance. These can provide early alerts about proposed legislation affecting freelance income.
• Follow industry news related to writing, publishing, and freelancing. Sometimes, tax changes specifically target these sectors, and staying in the loop can give you a heads-up.

Understand the Impacts of New Laws:
• When new tax laws are proposed or enacted, take the time to understand how they might affect you. For example, a change in the tax treatment of business expenses could impact how you deduct costs related to your writing.
• Consider how broader economic policies might influence your taxes. For example, shifts in income tax brackets or changes to capital gains taxes could alter

your financial strategies.

Consult with a Tax Professional:

• Regular consultations with a tax advisor can help you navigate upcoming changes. A tax professional can offer personalized advice based on your specific situation and help you adjust your strategies as needed.

• If you're unsure how a new law affects you, don't hesitate to ask for clarification. It's better to be proactive than to discover an unexpected tax liability later.

Anticipating Changes in Deductions and Credits

One of the most significant ways tax laws can change is through adjustments to deductions and credits. As an author, many of your deductions might be subject to changes in tax law.

For example:

• **Home Office Deduction:** This deduction has been a hot topic in recent years, with varying rules depending on whether you're self-employed or working as an employee. Future changes could expand or restrict eligibility, so keep an eye on this one if you work from home.

If you learn that the home office deduction might be limited, you could front-load related expenses, such as equipment purchases, to take advantage of the current rules.

- **Education and Professional Development:** Credits and deductions related to continuing education might change, affecting how much you can deduct for courses, workshops, or conferences.

- **Health Insurance Deduction:** If you're self-employed, changes in health insurance laws could impact the deductions available for your health insurance premiums.

Example: Preparing for Potential Tax Law Changes

Let's say there's talk of reducing the deduction for business travel expenses. As an author who frequently travels for book tours, conferences, and research, this change could significantly impact your taxes.

To prepare, you might:

- Accelerate planned travel before the law changes to take advantage of the current deduction.
- Explore other areas where you can maximize deductions, such as home office expenses or professional development.
- Adjust your budget to account for the potential increase in taxable income if the deduction is reduced or eliminated.

Adapting to Changes in Tax Rates

Changes in tax rates are another common way tax laws evolve. Whether it's income tax rates, capital gains taxes, or self-employment taxes, rate changes can affect your overall tax liability.

For example, if you anticipate a future increase in income tax rates, you might consider strategies like:

- **Deferring Income:** If possible, you could delay receiving certain income until a year when tax rates are lower.
- **Accelerating Deductions:** Conversely, you might accelerate deductions into the current year to reduce taxable income before rates increase.
- **Reevaluating Your Business Structure:** Changes in tax rates could make it advantageous to reconsider your business structure. For example, forming an LLC or S-Corp might offer tax benefits in a changing tax environment. (see Chapter Two)

The Importance of Flexibility

As with any good story, flexibility is key. The ability to adapt to new tax laws and adjust your financial strategies accordingly is essential. By staying informed, consulting with professionals, and planning for potential changes, you can ensure that your financial future is as well-written as your novels.

The Retirement Roadmap: Planning for the Future

Every author knows the importance of crafting a satisfying conclusion, and your financial life is no different. Planning for retirement is like plotting the final chapters of your career. It's about ensuring that you can enjoy the fruits of your labor without worrying about the next paycheck. In this section, we'll explore how to create a retirement roadmap that allows you to retire comfortably, whether you're planning to step back from writing entirely or simply slow down.

Starting with the End in Mind

Just like outlining a novel, retirement planning starts with envisioning the end goal. What does your ideal retirement look like? Do you see yourself living in a quiet countryside cottage, spending your days reading and writing at leisure? Or perhaps you dream of traveling the world, writing about your adventures? Whatever your vision, your retirement plan should be tailored to support it.

Understanding Retirement Accounts

There are several types of retirement accounts to consider, each with its own tax implications.

Here's a quick overview of the most common options

Traditional IRA (Individual Retirement Account):

• Contributions to a traditional IRA are often tax-deductible, which means they reduce your taxable income in the year you make them. However, you'll pay taxes on the money when you withdraw it in retirement.
• Traditional IRAs are a good option if you expect to be in a lower tax bracket in retirement than you are now.

Roth IRA:

• With a Roth IRA, contributions are made with after-tax dollars, so you won't get a tax deduction upfront. However, the money grows tax-free, and you can withdraw it tax-free in retirement.
• Roth IRAs are ideal if you expect to be in the same or a higher tax bracket in retirement, or if you want the flexibility of tax-free income later in life.

SEP IRA (Simplified Employee Pension):

• A SEP IRA is a type of retirement plan designed for self-employed individuals and small business owners. Contributions are tax-deductible, and the account offers high contribution limits compared to traditional and Roth IRAs.

• If you're earning a significant income from your writing, a SEP IRA can help you save more for retirement while reducing your current tax liability.

Solo 401(k):

• A Solo 401(k) is another retirement plan option for self-employed individuals. It allows for both employee and employer contributions, meaning you can save a larger portion of your income.

• Like a traditional 401(k), contributions are tax-deductible, and the money grows tax-deferred until you withdraw it in retirement.

Creating a Sustainable Income Stream

In addition to your retirement accounts, consider other sources of income that can provide financial stability in retirement.

These might include:

• **Royalties from Book Sales:** If your books continue to sell well, royalties can provide a steady stream of income in retirement. Keep in mind that royalties are taxable, so plan accordingly.

- **Passive Income Streams:** Consider diversifying your income with passive income sources, such as investments in dividend-paying stocks, rental properties, or other ventures that require minimal ongoing effort.
- **Downsizing or Relocating:** If your retirement vision includes a change of scenery, downsizing your home or moving to a lower-cost area could free up additional funds for your retirement years.

Example: Crafting Your Retirement Story

Let's say you're planning to retire in 10 years. You currently have a traditional IRA and a Roth IRA, along with a SEP IRA that you contribute to regularly.

To create a sustainable retirement plan, you might:

- Increase your contributions to the SEP IRA while you're still earning a high income, maximizing your tax deductions and building a larger nest egg.
- Continue contributing to your Roth IRA, allowing it to grow tax-free and providing you with a source of tax-free income in retirement.
- As you near retirement, work with a financial advisor to develop a withdrawal strategy that minimizes taxes, taking RMDs from your traditional IRA first and letting your Roth IRA grow.
- Plan for other income sources, such as royalties from your books, to supplement your retirement savings.

Chapter Fourteen

Resources and Tools

Navigating taxes might seem like venturing into uncharted territory for most authors. But just like your manuscripts, with the right plot twist, you can avoid financial pitfalls.

Managing finances on your own is commendable, but there comes a point in every author's journey when consulting a professional isn't just helpful, it's essential.

When Should You Seek Professional Help?

So, when is it time to call in the pros? Here are some scenarios where professional help can be a game-changer:

Complex Tax Situations:

• If your tax situation involves more than just reporting book sales and royalties, such as income from speaking engagements, freelance writing, or advances, it's a good idea to consult a professional. They can help you navigate these complexities and ensure you're not missing out on deductions or credits.

• Income from book sales is straightforward, but the addition of speaking gigs, freelance projects, or advances can complicate your tax return. For instance, did you know that expenses related to author appearances at conferences could be deductible? A professional can help you take advantage of such deductions.

International Sales:

• Selling books internationally can introduce a host of tax complications, including different tax laws, withholding taxes, and currency exchange issues. An expert can help you understand your obligations and how to minimize your tax burden.

Starting a New Business:

• If you're branching out, maybe opening a small press, offering consulting services, or launching a writing course, you'll need to understand the tax implications. A tax professional can guide you on the best business structure and help you with the necessary filings

Audits and IRS Correspondence:

• Receiving a letter from the IRS can be nerve-wracking. Whether it's an audit notice or a request for more information, having a professional on your side can ensure you respond appropriately and avoid further complications.

Major Life Changes:

• Getting married, divorced, having children, or moving to a new state can all affect your taxes. A tax advisor can help you understand these changes and adjust your tax strategy accordingly.

• Planning for the future and bequeathing royalties is best discussed with an attorney who specializes in estate planning.

Benefits of Consulting a Professional

Why should you bring in an expert? Here are a few reasons:

• **Peace of Mind:** Just like knowing your manuscript is in good hands with a trusted editor, working with a tax professional can give you peace of mind that your finances are being handled correctly.

• **Maximizing Deductions:** Professionals are well-versed in the deductions and credits available to authors, which means they can help you keep more of your hard-earned money.

- **Saving Time:** Tax professionals can handle the complex and time-consuming tasks, freeing you up to focus on your writing.
- **Avoiding Mistakes:** A self-employed author might mistakenly classify a writing retreat as a vacation. A tax pro would ensure it's listed correctly as a business expense, keeping you on the right side of the law

Finding the Right Professional: CPAs and Tax Attorneys

Now that you know when to seek help, the next step is finding the right professional. There are two main types of experts you might consider: Certified Public Accountants (CPAs) and tax attorneys. Think of CPAs as your tax-savvy advisors for day-to-day business and tax planning, while tax attorneys are like your legal knights, ready to defend you in battle against IRS audits or disputes.

Certified Public Accountants (CPAs)

A CPA is like the Swiss Army knife of tax professionals. They're trained in a wide range of financial areas, from tax preparation and planning to auditing and consulting. Here's why you might choose a CPA:

- **Tax Preparation and Filing:** CPAs are experts in preparing and filing tax returns. They know the ins and outs of tax law and can help you claim all the deductions and credits you're entitled to.

- **Tax Planning:** A CPA can help you develop a tax strategy that minimizes your liability and maximizes your savings, **both** now and in the future.
- **Business Consulting:** If you're running a business or planning to start one, a CPA can offer valuable advice on business structure, financial planning, and more.
- **Bookkeeping Services:** Many CPAs also offer bookkeeping services, which can be a huge help in keeping your financial records organized throughout the year.

Tax Attorneys

A tax attorney is your go-to expert when you're facing legal issues related to your taxes. While they can also help with tax planning and preparation, their expertise shines in areas like:

- **Legal Representation:** If you're facing an audit, tax dispute, or legal issue with the IRS, a tax attorney can represent you and negotiate on your behalf. (Warning: tax attorneys can be very expensive, so be mindful of who you choose).
- **Tax Litigation:** If your tax issue escalates to the point of litigation, a tax attorney is the professional who will represent you in court.
- **Complex Tax Issues:** For issues involving international taxes, estate planning, or significant amounts of money, a tax attorney's specialized knowledge can be invaluable.

Choosing the Right Professional

So, how do you decide between a CPA and a tax attorney? Here are a few tips:

- **For Routine Tax Matters:** If you're looking for help with tax preparation, filing, and general financial advice, a CPA is usually the best choice. They're well-equipped to handle most tax situations that authors face.
- **For Legal Issues:** If you're dealing with a tax dispute, audit, or legal issue, a tax attorney is your best bet. They can provide legal advice and represent you in dealings with the IRS.
- **For Business and Tax Planning:** Both CPAs and tax attorneys can help with tax planning, but CPAs are often more accessible and affordable for day-to-day tax advice and business consulting.

Overview of Tax Software

In the digital age, tax software can be a lifesaver for self-published authors. These programs are designed to simplify the tax filing process, guiding you through each step and helping you claim deductions specific to your business. Here's a look at some of the most popular tax software options and how they can help you manage your author finances.

TurboTax

TurboTax is one of the most popular tax software options out there, and for good reason. It's user-friendly and offers a range of features that can help self-published authors navigate their tax returns with ease.

- **Guided Tax Preparation:** TurboTax walks you through the tax filing process step-by-step, asking questions about your income, expenses, and deductions. This makes it easy to ensure you're not missing anything important.
- **Deduction Finder:** TurboTax is great at identifying deductions that self-employed individuals, like authors, can claim. It covers everything from home office expenses to business travel.
- **Self-Employed Edition:** The Self-Employed edition of TurboTax is specifically designed for freelancers and self-employed individuals, offering features tailored to your needs, such as estimating quarterly tax payments and tracking business expenses.

H&R Block

H&R Block is another well-known tax software provider that offers a range of options for self-published authors.

- **In-Person Support:** One of the standout features of H&R Block is its network of physical locations. If you start your return online but get stuck, you can visit an office for in-person help.

- **Freelancer Edition:** H&R Block's Freelancer edition is designed for self-employed individuals and includes features like expense tracking, tax deduction identification, and easy import of income data from various sources.
- **Audit Support:** H&R Block offers audit support, meaning that if you're audited by the IRS, they'll provide guidance and help you respond.

TaxAct

TaxAct is a more budget-friendly option that still offers robust features for self-published authors.

- **Affordable Pricing:** TaxAct is known for its competitive pricing, making it a good choice if you're looking to save money on tax preparation.
- **Self-Employed Edition:** Like other software, TaxAct has a Self-Employed edition that's tailored to the needs of freelancers and self-employed individuals. It includes tools for tracking income and expenses and identifying deductions.
- **Accuracy Guarantee:** TaxAct offers an accuracy guarantee, promising to cover any costs incurred due to errors in their software.

QuickBooks Self-Employed

While primarily known as accounting software, QuickBooks Self-Employed also offers tax preparation features that can be a great asset for authors.

• **Expense Tracking:** QuickBooks Self-Employed automatically tracks your expenses and categorizes them for tax purposes. This makes it easy to see where your money is going and identify potential deductions.
• **Mileage Tracking:** If you drive for work-related purposes, QuickBooks Self-Employed includes a mileage tracker to help you claim this deduction.
• **Tax Filing:** QuickBooks Self-Employed integrates with TurboTax, allowing you to export your financial data directly into your tax return.

Choosing the Right Software

When choosing tax software, consider the following:

• **Ease of Use:** If you're not a tax expert, choose software that's user-friendly and offers plenty of guidance.
• **Cost:** Compare the pricing of different software options to find one that fits your budget. Keep in mind that more expensive options often include more features or better support.
• **Features:** Consider what features are most important to you, whether it's expense tracking, deduction identification, or the ability to file both federal and state taxes.

Additional Tools for Financial Management

Beyond tax software, there are several other tools that can help you manage your finances as an author. These tools can help you keep track of your income and expenses, budget effectively, and plan for the future.

Budgeting Tools

Budgeting is a key part of managing your finances, especially if your income fluctuates throughout the year. Here are some tools that can help you create and stick to a budget:

- **You Need a Budget (YNAB):** YNAB is a popular budgeting tool that's designed to help you take control of your money. It focuses on helping you break the paycheck-to-paycheck cycle.
- **PocketGuard:** PocketGuard is another budgeting app that helps you track your spending and save money. It shows you how much you have left to spend after accounting for bills and goals, helping you avoid overspending.
- If budgeting consistency is your Achilles' heel, YNAB encourages you to 'give every dollar a job,' while PocketGuard shows you how much spending money you have left after accounting for bills.

Expense Tracking Tools

Keeping track of your expenses is crucial for both budgeting and tax purposes. Here are some tools that can help:

- **Expensify:** Expensify is a popular tool for tracking expenses, particularly for business purposes. It allows you to scan receipts, track mileage, and categorize expenses, making it easier to claim deductions at tax time.
- **Shoeboxed:** Shoeboxed is another expense tracking tool that's great for organizing receipts. You can scan receipts using their app or send them in via mail, and Shoeboxed will categorize them for you.
- **Wave:** Wave offers free accounting software that includes expense tracking features. It's designed for small businesses and freelancers, making it a good fit for self-published authors.

Financial Planning Tools

For long-term financial planning, consider these tools:

- **Personal Capital:** Personal Capital is a financial planning tool that helps you track your net worth, manage investments, and plan for retirement. It offers a comprehensive view of your finances, making it easier to set and achieve financial goals.
- **NewRetirement:** NewRetirement is a retirement planning tool that helps you create a detailed retirement

plan. It's particularly useful if you're looking to ensure you have enough saved to retire comfortably.

- **Tiller:** Tiller is a financial planning tool that integrates with Google Sheets to create customizable budgeting and financial planning spreadsheets. It's a good option if you like having control over your financial data and want to create your own reports.

- **Tiller:** Tiller is a financial planning tool that integrates with Google Sheets to create customizable budgeting and financial planning spreadsheets. It's a good option if you

Conclusion

And so, we've reached the final chapter of our financial tale. A story not just of numbers and forms, but of empowerment, strategy, and taking control of your writing career in ways that go beyond the keyboard. Like any good story, we've had twists, turns, and maybe a few plot holes along the way (we blame the IRS for those). But here you are, standing at the end with a wealth of knowledge ready to be applied to your author life.

From Rough Draft to Polished Plan

Your bookkeeping skills might be rough around the edges at first, but with some editing, research, and maybe a bit of outside help, they can turn into something you can be proud of. The tools, tips, and strategies we've explored together are your editing tools, there to cut the fluff, enhance the good bits, and make sure every chapter of your financial story is working toward your ultimate goal: keeping more of what you earn.

Plotting Your Financial Future

Just as every good book leaves room for a sequel, your financial journey doesn't end here. There are always new tax laws to consider, new income streams to explore, and new strategies to implement. But now, you're equipped with the knowledge to navigate these changes with confidence. Whether you're writing your next bestseller or planning your retirement, you've got the skills to make sure your finances are as sharp as your prose.

The Author's Final Word

As you close this book (or perhaps just scroll to the top to revisit your favorite chapter), remember that managing your finances is an ongoing process, much like writing itself. It's not always easy, and sometimes the best advice is to step away and let a professional take a look. But with the right tools, a bit of planning, and a touch of creativity, you can master the business side of your writing career without losing sight of why you started writing in the first place.

The IRS may not be your biggest fan, but with the right financial tools, you can still write your own tax tale. One that doesn't end with 'and then the penalties came.'

Here's to your continued success, both in your writing and in keeping the taxman at bay. May your stories captivate readers, your royalties overflow, and your tax returns always have a happy ending.

Now, take a deep breath, review your finances, and decide which resources you need. Remember, your time is better spent crafting your next bestseller than worrying over tax returns!

Frustrated by another incomplete book? Learn new ways to escape the hamster wheel and fill the shelves with brilliant best-sellers.

Has your dream of authorship turned into a collection of half-finished manuscripts? Inspired by a great idea only to face burnout in the messy middle? Are you terrified by the evils of editing? **Start reading *Extreme Planning for Authors* to craft a must-read today!**

Thank You!

Thank you so much for enjoying *Write it Off!* If you've enjoyed the book, please consider leaving a review, to help other readers find this resource.

Giving a review to an author is like the applause at the end of a concert, and authors greatly appreciate them!

If you would like to get updates, sneak previews, sales, and FREE STUFF, please sign up for my newsletter.
http://www.greendragonartist.com/about/ newsletter

**See all the books available through Green Dragon Publishing at
http://www.greendragonartist.com/books**

Appendices

Glossary of Tax Terms: Common Tax Terminology

Navigating tax terminology can feel like trying to read an ancient manuscript in a foreign language. Here's a glossary of common tax terms that will help you decode the tax world without needing a translator.

Asset: Anything of value owned by a business or individual, such as cash, equipment, or property.

Capital Gain: The profit earned from selling an asset for more than its purchase price. If you sell a book for more than you paid to publish it, that's a capital gain.

Credit: An amount that reduces your tax liability directly. Unlike deductions, which lower your taxable income, credits cut your tax bill dollar for dollar.

Deduction: Expenses that you can subtract from your gross income to reduce your taxable income.

Expense: A cost incurred in the process of earning income or operating a business, such as office supplies or travel expenses.

Equity: The difference between what you own (assets) and what you owe (liabilities). Equity represents your ownership stake in a business or property.

Estimated Taxes: Quarterly payments made to cover your tax liability throughout the year, rather than one lump sum at tax time.

Liability: An obligation or debt that a business or individual owes to others, such as loans or unpaid bills.

Net Income: The total income remaining after all expenses, deductions, and taxes have been subtracted.

Revenue: The total income generated from sales or services before any expenses are subtracted.

Schedule C: The form used to report income and expenses for a Sole Proprietorship. If you're self-employed or running a side gig, Schedule C is your go-to guide for detailing your business finances.

Self-Employment Tax: A tax consisting of Social Security and Medicare taxes primarily for individuals who work for themselves.

Tax Bracket: The range of income taxed at a specific rate. The higher your income, the higher your bracket and the more you're taxed. The higher tax bracket only applies to that amount of income above the defined tax 'ledge.'

Tax Liability: The total amount of tax you owe to the government.

Write-Off: Another term for a deduction. It's an expense you can subtract from your income to lower your taxable income.

List of Tax Forms: A Practical Guide

When it's time to tackle your taxes, the forms and instructions can seem like a maze. But we've got you covered with a guide to some of the most commonly used tax forms and how to navigate them.

Sole Proprietorship

Form 1040: U.S. Individual Income Tax Return

- Purpose: This is the primary form used to file your federal income tax return.
- Instructions: For sole proprietors, this form includes reporting business income and expenses on Schedule C.

Schedule C (Form 1040): Profit or Loss from Business

- Purpose: Used to report income and expenses for a Sole Proprietorship.
- Instructions: Detail your business income, deductions, and expenses. This form helps calculate your net profit or loss, which is then reported on your Form 1040.

Schedule SE (Form 1040): Self-Employment Tax

- Purpose: Used to calculate the self-employment tax due for Social Security and Medicare.
- Instructions: Based on the net income from Schedule C, this form helps determine how much self-employment tax you owe.

Partnership

Form 1065: U.S. Return of Partnership Income

• Purpose: This form is used to report the income, gains, losses, deductions, and credits from a Partnership.
• Instructions: Partnerships must file Form 1065 to report their financial activities. Each partner receives a Schedule K-1 to report their share of income or loss on their individual tax return.

Schedule K-1 (Form 1065): Partner's Share of Income, Deductions, Credits, etc.

• Purpose: Each partner receives this form, which details their share of the Partnership's income, deductions, and credits.
• Instructions: The information from Schedule K-1 is used by each partner to complete their individual tax return.

Corporation

Form 1120: U.S. Corporation Income Tax Return

- Purpose: This form is used by Corporations to report their income, gains, losses, deductions, and credits.
- Instructions: Corporations must file Form 1120 annually. It details the Corporation's financial position and calculates the income tax due.

S Corporation

Form 1120-S: U.S. Income Tax Return for an S Corporation

- Purpose: This form is used to report income, deductions, and credits for S Corporations.
- Instructions: Similar to Form 1065 for Partnerships, S Corporations file Form 1120-S and issue Schedule K-1 to each shareholder. Shareholders use this form to report their share of the S Corporation's income, deductions, and credits on their individual tax returns.

Schedule K-1 (Form 1120-S): Shareholder's Share of Income, Deductions, Credits, etc.

- Purpose: Details each shareholder's share of the S Corporation's income, deductions, and credits.
- Instructions: The information from Schedule K-1 is used by shareholders to complete their individual tax returns.

Limited Liability Company (LLC)

Single-Member LLC:

Form 1040: U.S. Individual Income Tax Return

• Purpose: Single-member LLCs are treated as Sole Proprietorships for tax purposes. Income and expenses are reported on Schedule C attached to Form 1040.
• Instructions: Report LLC income and expenses on Schedule C, and file with your personal income tax return.

Multi-Member LLC:

Form 1065: U.S. Return of Partnership Income

• Purpose: Multi-member LLCs are generally treated as Partnerships for tax purposes. Use Form 1065 to report the LLC's income and expenses.
• Instructions: Similar to Partnerships, multi-member LLCs must file Form 1065 and provide each member with a Schedule K-1.

Schedule K-1 (Form 1065): Partner's Share of Income, Deductions, Credits, etc.

- Purpose: Used by each member of the LLC to report their share of the LLC's income, deductions, and credits.
- Instructions: Each member uses Schedule K-1 information to complete their individual tax returns.

Other

Form 1099-MISC: Miscellaneous Income

- Purpose: Reports various types of income, including freelance income, rental income, and more.
- Instructions: Fill this form if you've received income not reported on a W-2. It's like adding footnotes to your financial narrative to ensure all sources of income are documented.

Form W-2: Wage and Tax Statement

- Purpose: Reports wages paid and taxes withheld from your paycheck by your employer.
- Instructions: Your employer provides this form. Use it to confirm the accuracy of your reported income and withholdings. It's the confirmation page of your income story, ensuring everything adds up.

Books, Websites, and Articles for Further Reading

If you're looking to dive deeper into the world of taxes and financial management, here are some recommended resources:

IRS Website www.irs.gov
The official site for tax forms, instructions, and resources.
TaxAct Blog

Offers tips and updates on tax issues. It's like a writer's blog, providing insights and advice on navigating tax challenges.
• Nolo: Legal and Tax Information
A resource for legal and tax information, including guides and articles.
Small Business Association: www.sba.gov
Avalara Sales Tax Nexus by State www.avalara.com/us/en/learn/guides/sales-tax-nexus-laws-by-state.html

With these resources at your disposal, you're equipped to continue your journey through the tax landscape with confidence. Whether you're diving into state tax laws, exploring further reading, or joining a professional network, remember that mastering your finances is a process—a story that, with the right tools and knowledge, can have a truly satisfying conclusion. Happy writing, and here's to many more successful chapters in your financial and literary adventures!

About the Author

Christy Nicholas writes under several pen names, including Emeline Rhys, CN Jackson, and Rowan Dillon. She is an author, artist, and accountant. After she failed to become an airline pilot, she quit her ceaseless pursuit of careers that began with the letter 'A' and decided to concentrate on her writing. Since she has Project Completion Compulsion, she is one of the few authors with no unfinished novels.

Christy has her hands in many crafts, including digital art, beaded jewelry, writing, and photography. In real life, she's a CPA, but having grown up with art all around her (her mother, grandmother, and great-grandmother are/were all artists), it sort of infected her, as it were.

She wants to expose the incredible beauty in this world, hidden beneath the everyday grime of familiarity and habit, and share it with others. She uses characters out of time and places infused with magic and myth, writing magical realism stories in both historical fantasy and time travel flavors.

Social Media Links:
Blog: www.GreenDragonArtist.net